DODGERS

P
ERNANDO VALENZUELA

YANKEES

P
RON GUIDRY

ORIOLES

1B
EDDIE MURRAY

REDS

1B-MGR
PETE ROSE

ROYALS

3B
GEORGE BRETT

METS

P
DWIGHT GOODEN

ROYALS

P
BRET SABERHAGEN

ORIOLES

SS
CAL RIPKEN

BRAVES

OF
DALE MURPHY

THE COMPLETE PICTURE COLLECTION

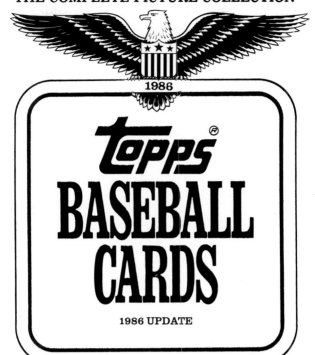

1986

Topps®
BASEBALL
CARDS

1986 UPDATE

THE COMPLETE PICTURE COLLECTION

1986

topps®
BASEBALL
CARDS

UPDATE 1986

Text by
Frank Slocum

Card History by
Sy Berger

WARNER BOOKS
Warner Communications Company

Warner Books Inc., 666 Fifth Avenue, New York, NY 10103
Ⓦ A Warner Communications Company

Designed and produced by MBKA, Inc.
Suite 8L, 340 East 80th Street, New York, NY 10021
Printed and bound in Hong Kong by
Mandarin Offset Marketing (HK) Ltd.
First Printing: November 1986
10 9 8 7 6 5 4 3 2 1

Library of Congress Cataloging-in-Publication Data

Slocum, Frank.
 Topps® baseball cards update, 1986.

 Continuation of: Topps baseball cards.
 1. Baseball cards—United States—Collectors and
collecting. I. Title.
GV875.3.S58 1986 769'.49796357'0973 86–40175
ISBN 0–446–51352–0

CONTENTS

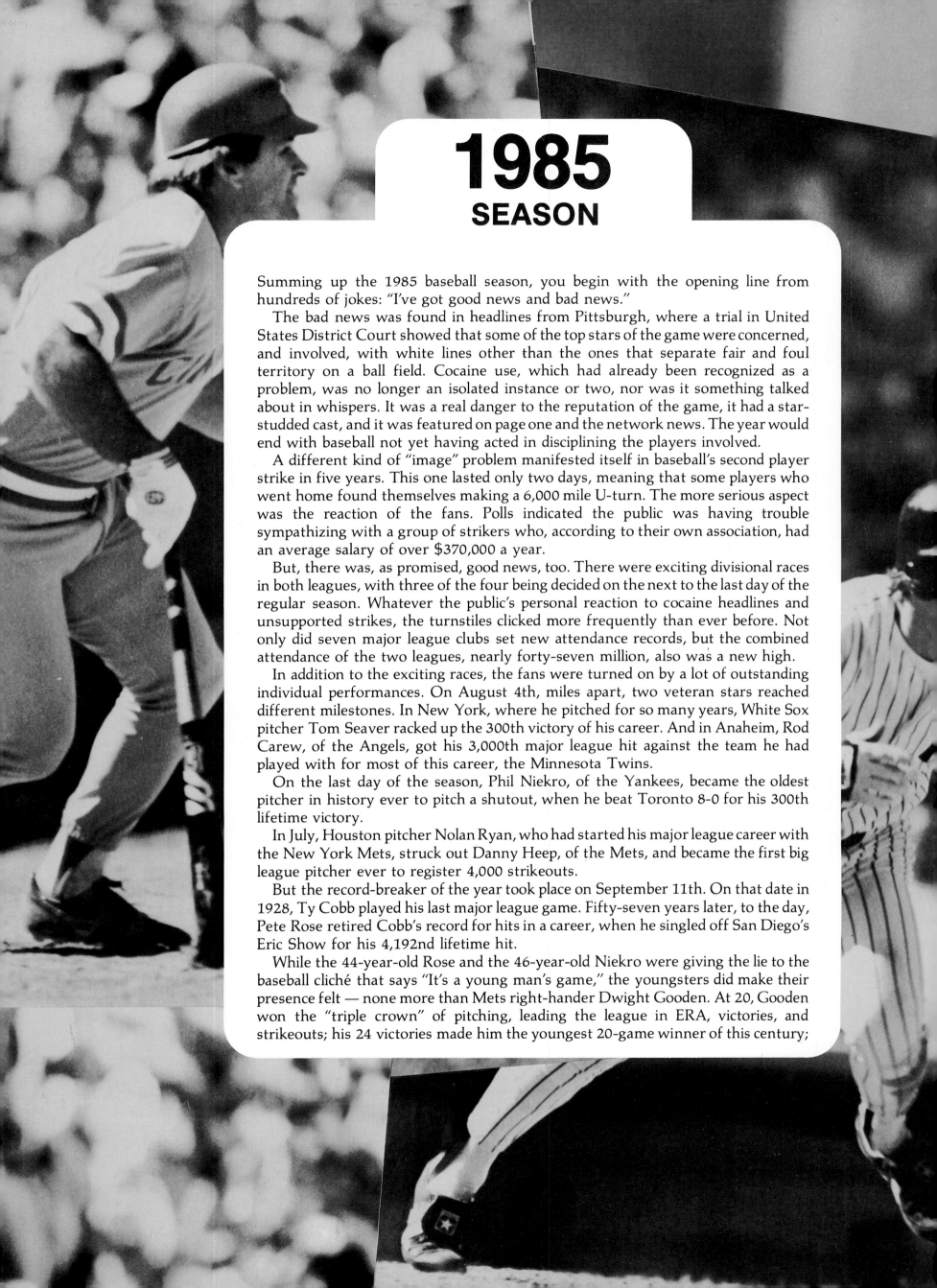

1985
SEASON

Summing up the 1985 baseball season, you begin with the opening line from hundreds of jokes: "I've got good news and bad news."

The bad news was found in headlines from Pittsburgh, where a trial in United States District Court showed that some of the top stars of the game were concerned, and involved, with white lines other than the ones that separate fair and foul territory on a ball field. Cocaine use, which had already been recognized as a problem, was no longer an isolated instance or two, nor was it something talked about in whispers. It was a real danger to the reputation of the game, it had a star-studded cast, and it was featured on page one and the network news. The year would end with baseball not yet having acted in disciplining the players involved.

A different kind of "image" problem manifested itself in baseball's second player strike in five years. This one lasted only two days, meaning that some players who went home found themselves making a 6,000 mile U-turn. The more serious aspect was the reaction of the fans. Polls indicated the public was having trouble sympathizing with a group of strikers who, according to their own association, had an average salary of over $370,000 a year.

But, there was, as promised, good news, too. There were exciting divisional races in both leagues, with three of the four being decided on the next to the last day of the regular season. Whatever the public's personal reaction to cocaine headlines and unsupported strikes, the turnstiles clicked more frequently than ever before. Not only did seven major league clubs set new attendance records, but the combined attendance of the two leagues, nearly forty-seven million, also was a new high.

In addition to the exciting races, the fans were turned on by a lot of outstanding individual performances. On August 4th, miles apart, two veteran stars reached different milestones. In New York, where he pitched for so many years, White Sox pitcher Tom Seaver racked up the 300th victory of his career. And in Anaheim, Rod Carew, of the Angels, got his 3,000th major league hit against the team he had played with for most of this career, the Minnesota Twins.

On the last day of the season, Phil Niekro, of the Yankees, became the oldest pitcher in history ever to pitch a shutout, when he beat Toronto 8-0 for his 300th lifetime victory.

In July, Houston pitcher Nolan Ryan, who had started his major league career with the New York Mets, struck out Danny Heep, of the Mets, and became the first big league pitcher ever to register 4,000 strikeouts.

But the record-breaker of the year took place on September 11th. On that date in 1928, Ty Cobb played his last major league game. Fifty-seven years later, to the day, Pete Rose retired Cobb's record for hits in a career, when he singled off San Diego's Eric Show for his 4,192nd lifetime hit.

While the 44-year-old Rose and the 46-year-old Niekro were giving the lie to the baseball cliché that says "It's a young man's game," the youngsters did make their presence felt — none more than Mets right-hander Dwight Gooden. At 20, Gooden won the "triple crown" of pitching, leading the league in ERA, victories, and strikeouts; his 24 victories made him the youngest 20-game winner of this century;

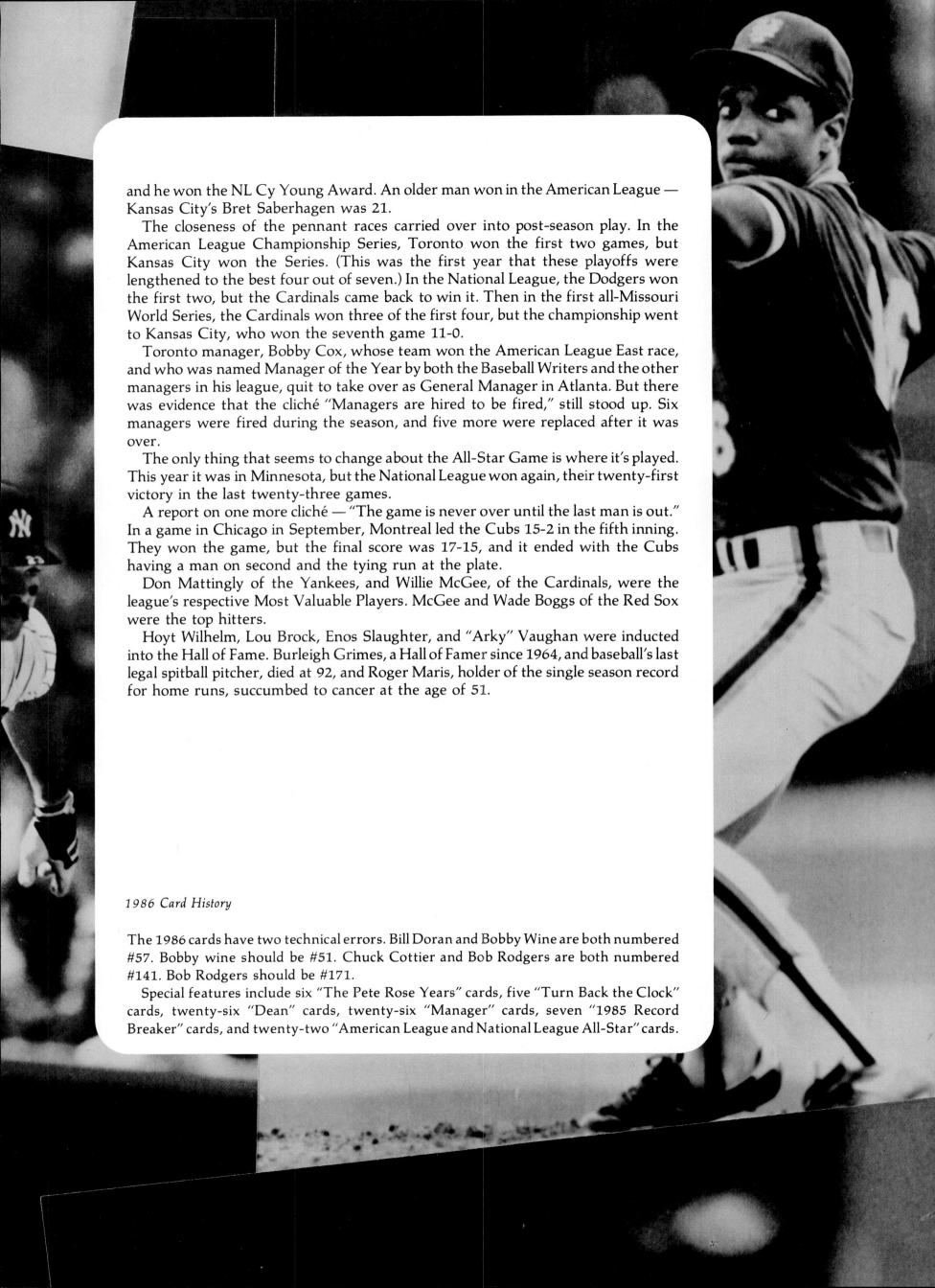

and he won the NL Cy Young Award. An older man won in the American League —
Kansas City's Bret Saberhagen was 21.

The closeness of the pennant races carried over into post-season play. In the
American League Championship Series, Toronto won the first two games, but
Kansas City won the Series. (This was the first year that these playoffs were
lengthened to the best four out of seven.) In the National League, the Dodgers won
the first two, but the Cardinals came back to win it. Then in the first all-Missouri
World Series, the Cardinals won three of the first four, but the championship went
to Kansas City, who won the seventh game 11-0.

Toronto manager, Bobby Cox, whose team won the American League East race,
and who was named Manager of the Year by both the Baseball Writers and the other
managers in his league, quit to take over as General Manager in Atlanta. But there
was evidence that the cliché "Managers are hired to be fired," still stood up. Six
managers were fired during the season, and five more were replaced after it was
over.

The only thing that seems to change about the All-Star Game is where it's played.
This year it was in Minnesota, but the National League won again, their twenty-first
victory in the last twenty-three games.

A report on one more cliché — "The game is never over until the last man is out."
In a game in Chicago in September, Montreal led the Cubs 15-2 in the fifth inning.
They won the game, but the final score was 17-15, and it ended with the Cubs
having a man on second and the tying run at the plate.

Don Mattingly of the Yankees, and Willie McGee, of the Cardinals, were the
league's respective Most Valuable Players. McGee and Wade Boggs of the Red Sox
were the top hitters.

Hoyt Wilhelm, Lou Brock, Enos Slaughter, and "Arky" Vaughan were inducted
into the Hall of Fame. Burleigh Grimes, a Hall of Famer since 1964, and baseball's last
legal spitball pitcher, died at 92, and Roger Maris, holder of the single season record
for home runs, succumbed to cancer at the age of 51.

1986 Card History

The 1986 cards have two technical errors. Bill Doran and Bobby Wine are both numbered
#57. Bobby wine should be #51. Chuck Cottier and Bob Rodgers are both numbered
#141. Bob Rodgers should be #171.

Special features include six "The Pete Rose Years" cards, five "Turn Back the Clock"
cards, twenty-six "Dean" cards, twenty-six "Manager" cards, seven "1985 Record
Breaker" cards, and twenty-two "American League and National League All-Star" cards.

TRADED SERIES 1985

ORIOLES
P
DON AASE

1T

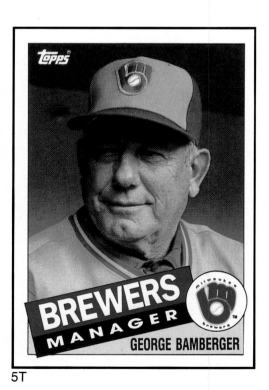

PIRATES
SS-OF
BILL ALMON

2T

INDIANS
OF
BENNY AYALA

3T

A's
OF-1B
DUSTY BAKER

4T

BREWERS
MANAGER
GEORGE BAMBERGER

5T

YANKEES
3B
DALE BERRA

6T

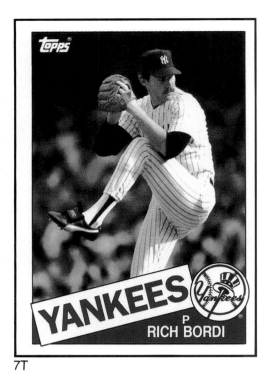

YANKEES
P
RICH BORDI

7T

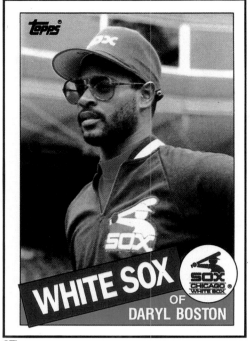

WHITE SOX
OF
DARYL BOSTON

8T

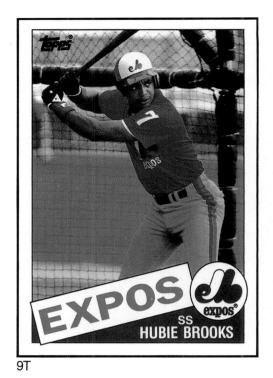

EXPOS
SS
HUBIE BROOKS

9T

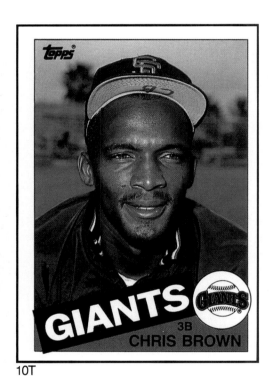

GIANTS
3B
CHRIS BROWN

10T

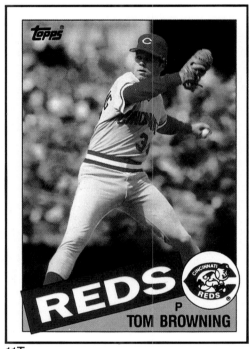

REDS
P
TOM BROWNING

11T

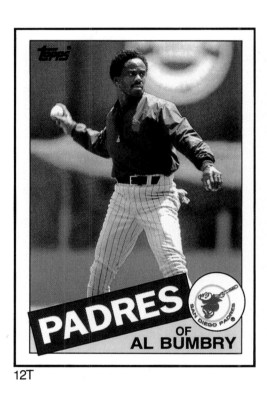

PADRES
OF
AL BUMBRY

12T

BREWERS
P
RAY BURRIS

13T

BLUE JAYS
DH
JEFF BURROUGHS

14T

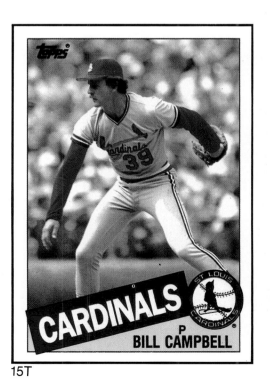

CARDINALS
P
BILL CAMPBELL

15T

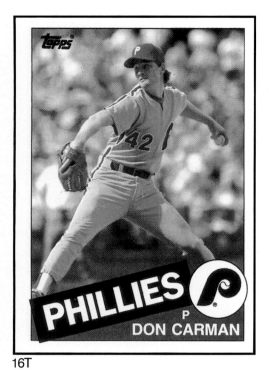

PHILLIES
P
DON CARMAN

16T

METS
C
GARY CARTER

17T

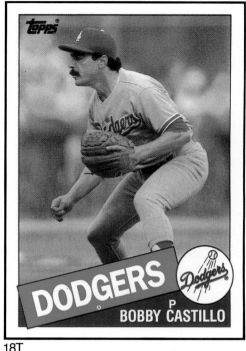

DODGERS
P
BOBBY CASTILLO

18T

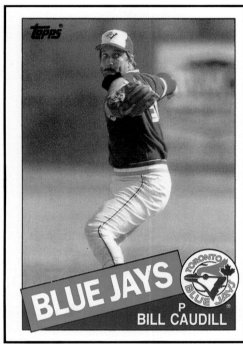

BLUE JAYS
P
BILL CAUDILL

19T

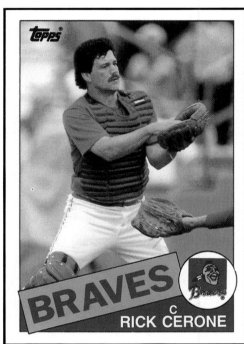

BRAVES
C
RICK CERONE

20T

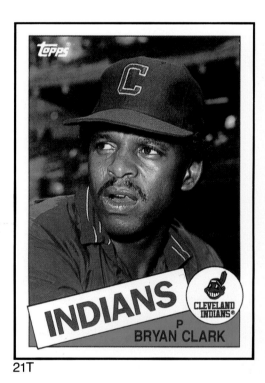

INDIANS
P
BRYAN CLARK

21T

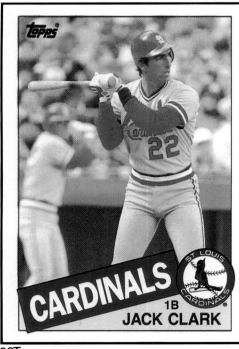

CARDINALS
1B
JACK CLARK

22T

ANGELS
P
PAT CLEMENTS

23T

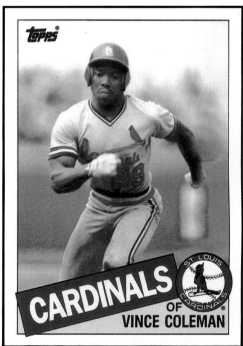

CARDINALS
OF
VINCE COLEMAN

24T

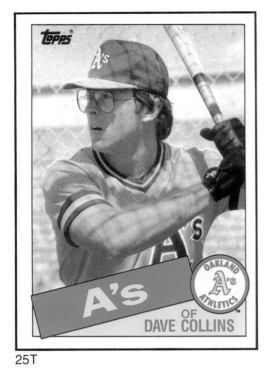

A's
OF DAVE COLLINS

25T

BREWERS
P DANNY DARWIN

26T

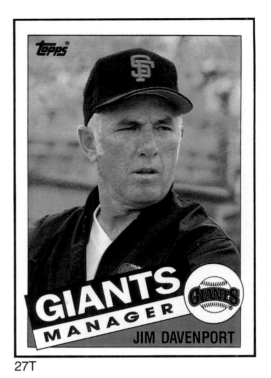

GIANTS
MANAGER JIM DAVENPORT

27T

PADRES
OF JERRY DAVIS

28T

CUBS
OF BRIAN DAYETT

29T

CARDINALS
SS IVAN DeJESUS

30T

ORIOLES
P KEN DIXON

31T

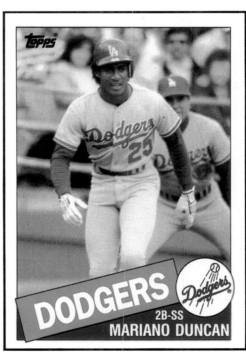

DODGERS
2B-SS MARIANO DUNCAN

32T

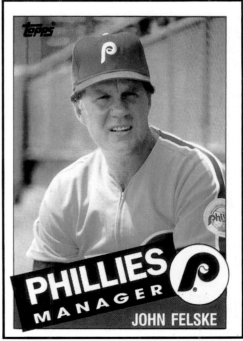

PHILLIES
MANAGER JOHN FELSKE

33T

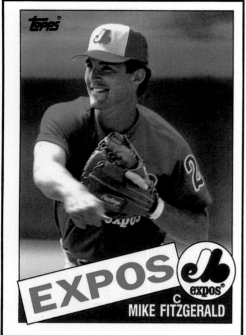

EXPOS
MIKE FITZGERALD

34T

CUBS
RAY FONTENOT

35T

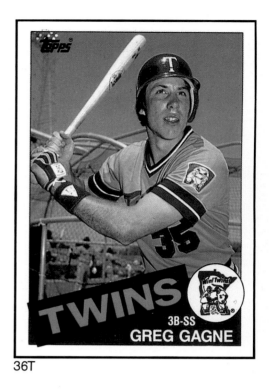

TWINS
3B-SS
GREG GAGNE

36T

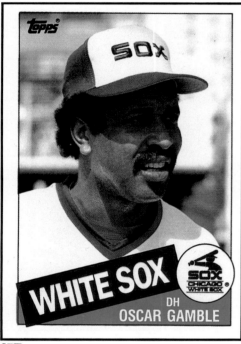

WHITE SOX
DH
OSCAR GAMBLE

37T

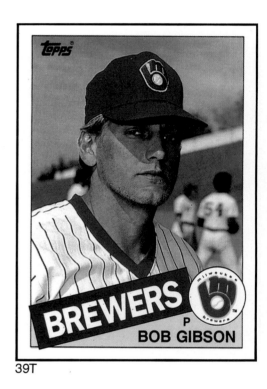

GIANTS
SCOTT GARRELTS

38T

BREWERS
BOB GIBSON

39T

GIANTS
JIM GOTT

40T

GIANTS
1B
DAVID GREEN

41T

A'S
SS
ALFREDO GRIFFIN

42T

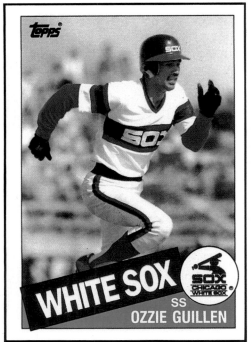

WHITE SOX
SS
OZZIE GUILLEN

43T

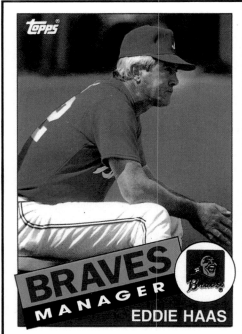

BRAVES
MANAGER
EDDIE HAAS

44T

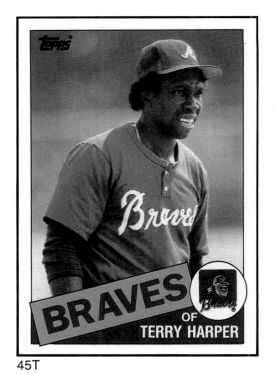

BRAVES
OF
TERRY HARPER

45T

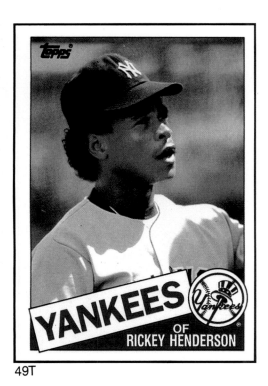

RANGERS
SS-2B
TOBY HARRAH

46T

RANGERS
P
GREG HARRIS

47T

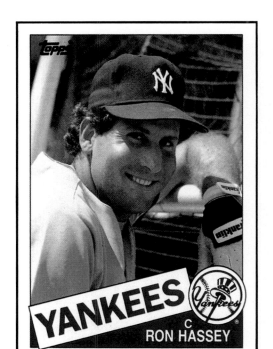

YANKEES
C
RON HASSEY

48T

YANKEES
OF
RICKEY HENDERSON

49T

A's
OF
STEVE HENDERSON

50T

PIRATES
OF
GEORGE HENDRICK

51T

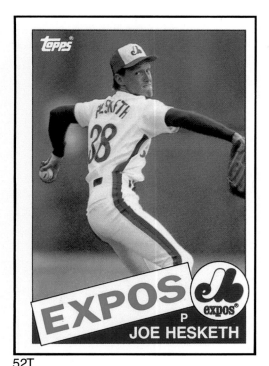

EXPOS
JOE HESKETH
52T

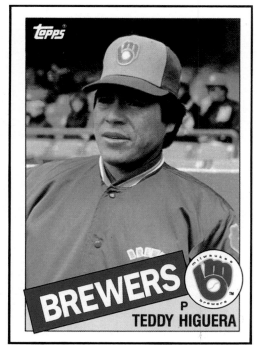

BREWERS
TEDDY HIGUERA
53T

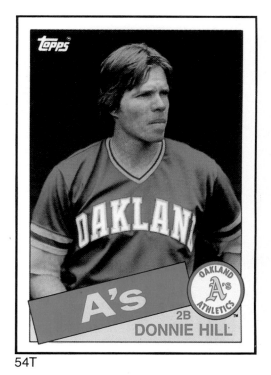

A's
DONNIE HILL
54T

PIRATES
AL HOLLAND
55T

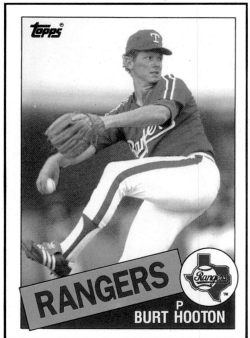

RANGERS
BURT HOOTON
56T

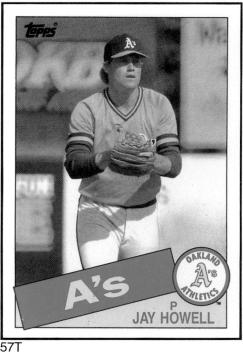

A's
JAY HOWELL
57T

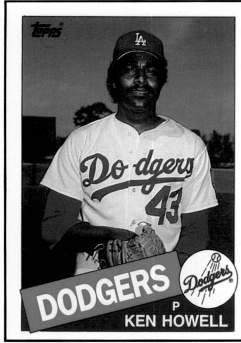

DODGERS
KEN HOWELL
58T

PADRES
LaMARR HOYT
59T

WHITE SOX
TIM HULETT
60T

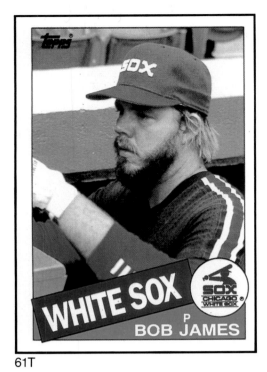

WHITE SOX

P
BOB JAMES

61T

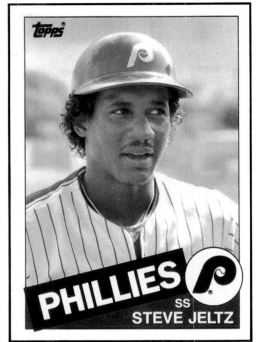

PHILLIES

SS
STEVE JELTZ

62T

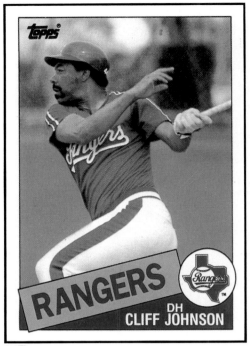

RANGERS

DH
CLIFF JOHNSON

63T

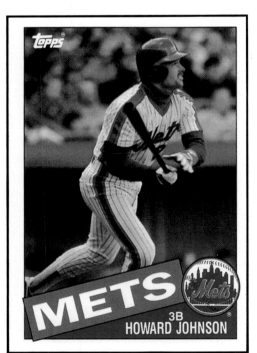

METS

3B
HOWARD JOHNSON

64T

ANGELS

OF
RUPPERT JONES

65T

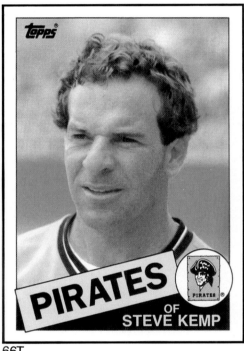

PIRATES

OF
STEVE KEMP

66T

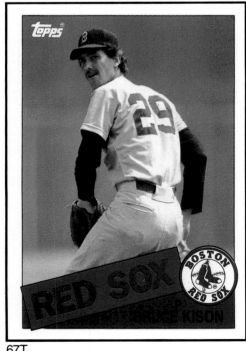

RED SOX

P
BRUCE KISON

67T

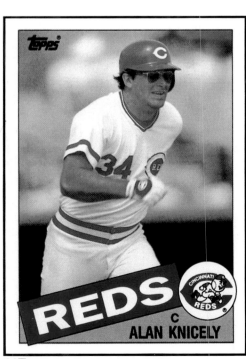

REDS

C
ALAN KNICELY

68T

ROYALS

P
MIKE LaCOSS

69T

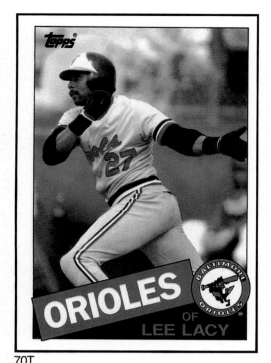

ORIOLES
OF
LEE LACY

70T

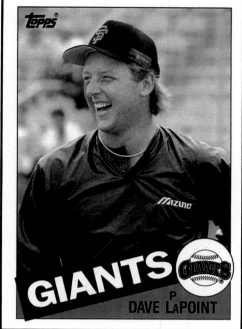

GIANTS
P
DAVE LaPOINT

71T

BLUE JAYS
P
GARY LAVELLE

72T

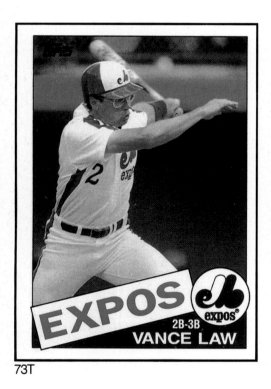

EXPOS
2B-3B
VANCE LAW

73T

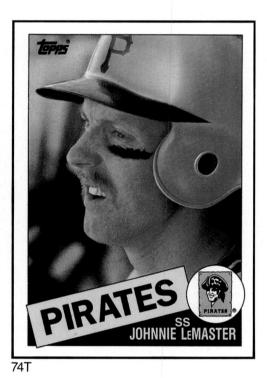

PIRATES
SS
JOHNNIE LeMASTER

74T

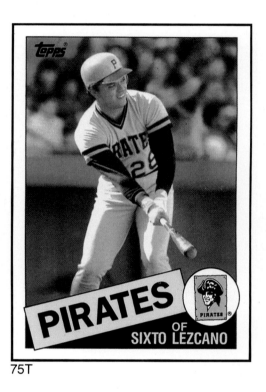

PIRATES
OF
SIXTO LEZCANO

75T

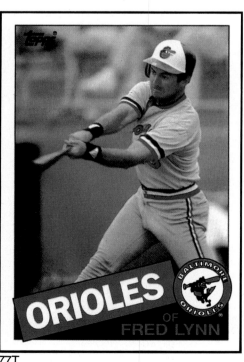

WHITE SOX
P
TIM LOLLAR

76T

ORIOLES
OF
FRED LYNN

77T

YANKEES
MANAGER
BILLY MARTIN

78T

ASTROS
P
RON MATHIS

79T

BLUE JAYS
DH
LEN MATUSZEK

80T

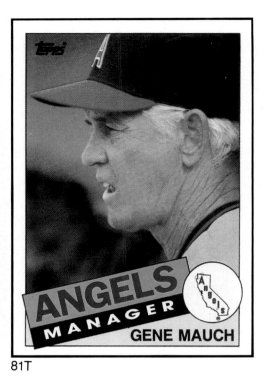

ANGELS
MANAGER
GENE MAUCH

81T

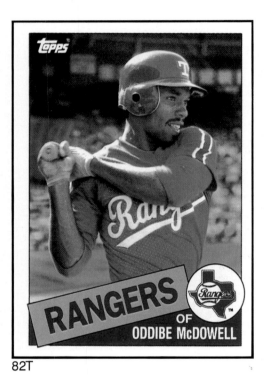

RANGERS
OF
ODDIBE McDOWELL

82T

METS
P
ROGER McDOWELL

83T

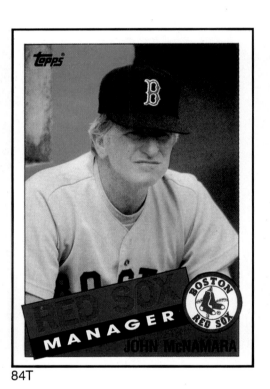

RED SOX
MANAGER
JOHN McNAMARA

84T

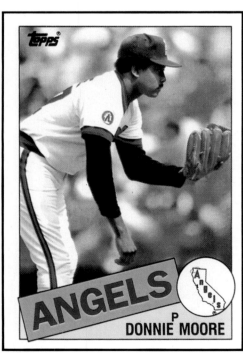

ANGELS
P
DONNIE MOORE

85T

WHITE SOX
P
GENE NELSON

86T

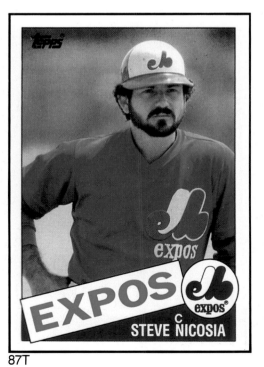

EXPOS
C
STEVE NICOSIA

87T

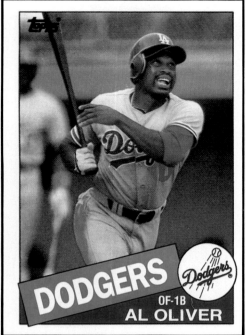

DODGERS OF-1B
AL OLIVER

88T

PIRATES OF
JOE ORSULAK

89T

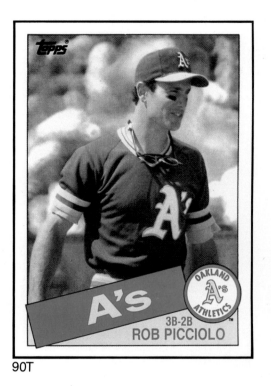

A's 3B-2B
ROB PICCIOLO

90T

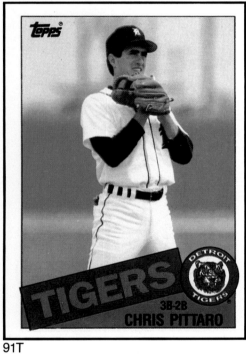

TIGERS 3B-2B
CHRIS PITTARO

91T

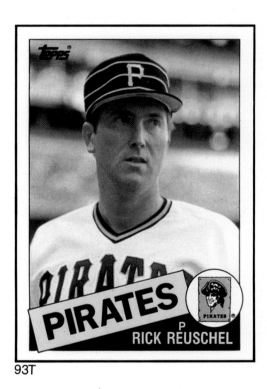

MARINERS 3B
JIM PRESLEY

92T

PIRATES P
RICK REUSCHEL

93T

EXPOS P
BERT ROBERGE

94T

EXPOS MANAGER
BOB RODGERS

95T

PADRES 2B
JERRY ROYSTER

96T

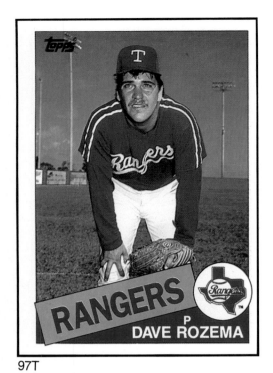

RANGERS
P
DAVE ROZEMA

97T

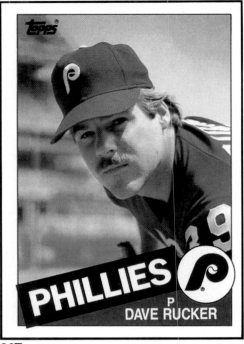

PHILLIES
P
DAVE RUCKER

98T

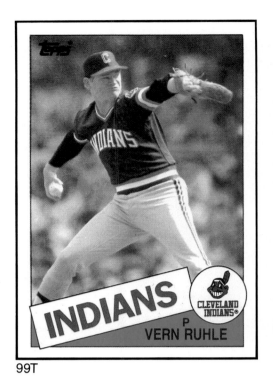

INDIANS
P
VERN RUHLE

99T

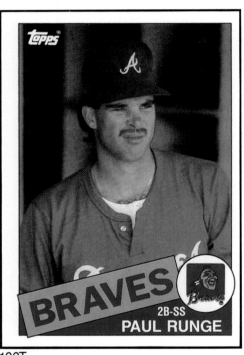

BRAVES
2B-SS
PAUL RUNGE

100T

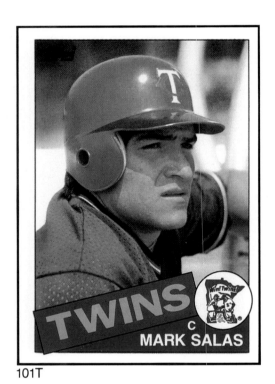

TWINS
C
MARK SALAS

101T

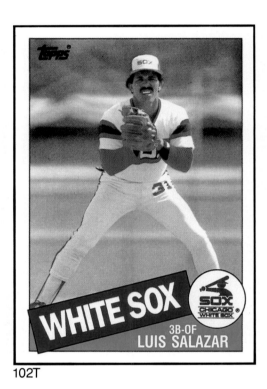

WHITE SOX
3B-OF
LUIS SALAZAR

102T

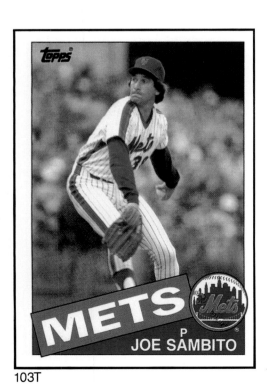

METS
P
JOE SAMBITO

103T

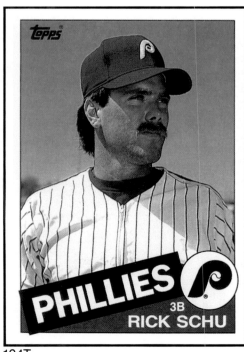

PHILLIES
3B
RICK SCHU

104T

MARINERS
C
DONNIE SCOTT

105T

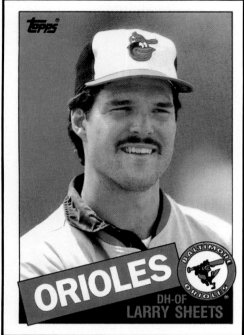

ORIOLES
DH-OF
LARRY SHEETS

106T

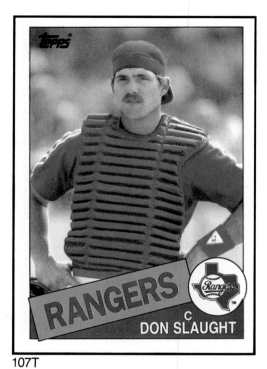

RANGERS
C
DON SLAUGHT

107T

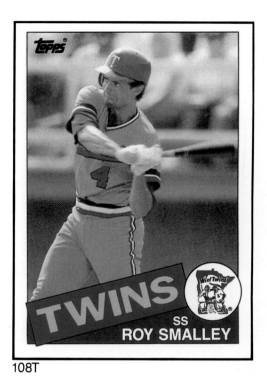

TWINS
SS
ROY SMALLEY

108T

ROYALS
OF
LONNIE SMITH

109T

ORIOLES
P
NATE SNELL

110T

CUBS
SS-2B
CHRIS SPEIER

111T

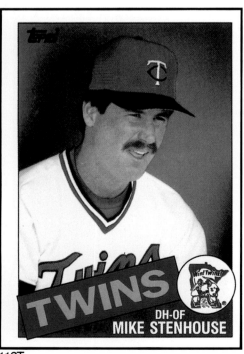

TWINS
DH-OF
MIKE STENHOUSE

112T

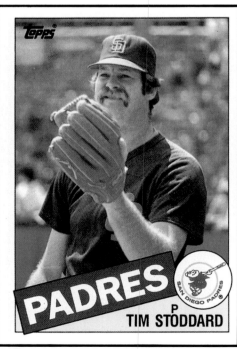

PADRES
P
TIM STODDARD

113T

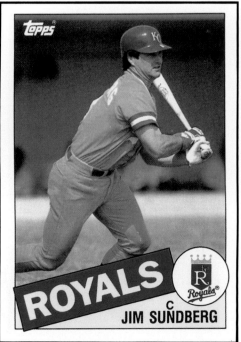

ROYALS
C
JIM SUNDBERG

114T

BRAVES
P
BRUCE SUTTER

115T

A's
P
DON SUTTON

116T

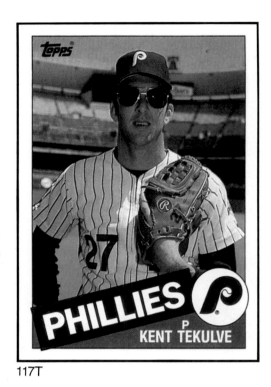

PHILLIES
P
KENT TEKULVE

117T

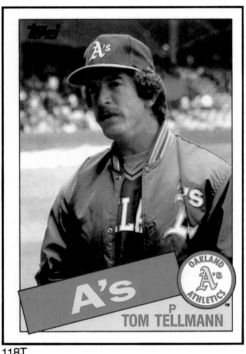

A's
P
TOM TELLMANN

118T

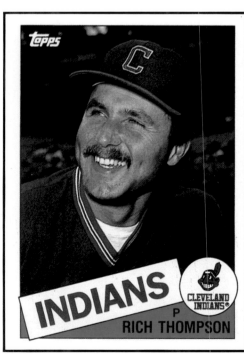

TIGERS
P
WALT TERRELL

119T

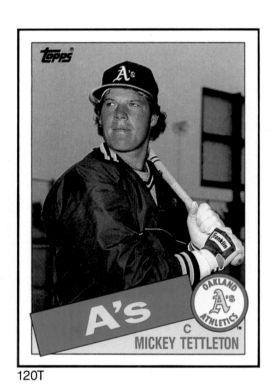

A's
C
MICKEY TETTLETON

120T

PHILLIES
SS-2B
DERREL THOMAS

121T

INDIANS
P
RICH THOMPSON

122T

GIANTS
C
ALEX TREVINO

123T

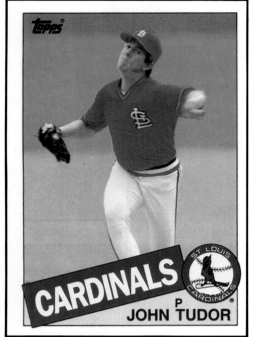

CARDINALS
P
JOHN TUDOR

124T

GIANTS
SS
JOSE URIBE

125T

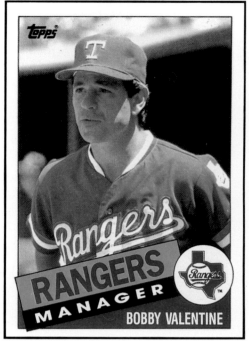

RANGERS
MANAGER
BOBBY VALENTINE

126T

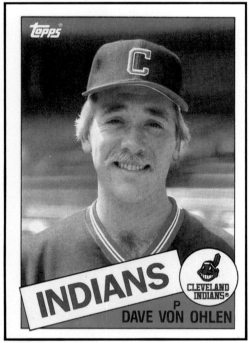

INDIANS
P
DAVE VON OHLEN

127T

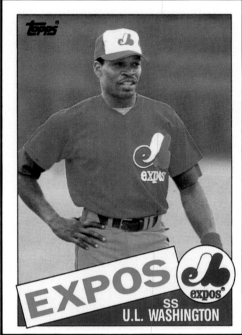

EXPOS
SS
U.L. WASHINGTON

128T

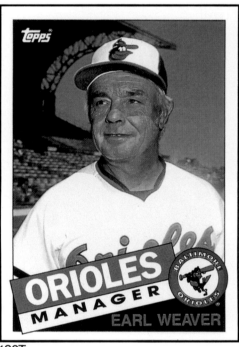

ORIOLES
MANAGER
EARL WEAVER

129T

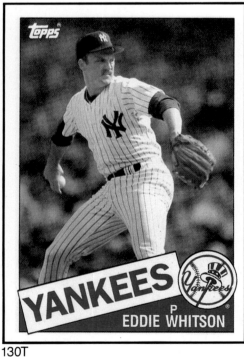

YANKEES
P
EDDIE WHITSON

130T

EXPOS
OF
HERM WINNINGHAM

131T

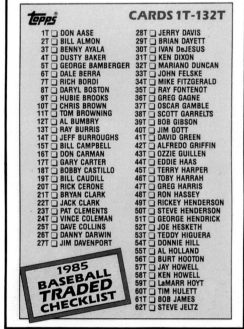

CARDS 1T-132T

1T	DON AASE	28T JERRY DAVIS
2T	BILL ALMON	29T BRIAN DAYETT
3T	BENNY AYALA	30T IVAN DeJESUS
4T	DUSTY BAKER	31T KEN DIXON
5T	GEORGE BAMBERGER	32T MARIANO DUNCAN
6T	DALE BERRA	33T JOHN FELSKE
7T	RICH BORDI	34T MIKE FITZGERALD
8T	DARYL BOSTON	35T RAY FONTENOT
9T	HUBIE BROOKS	36T GREG GAGNE
10T	CHRIS BROWN	37T OSCAR GAMBLE
11T	TOM BROWNING	38T SCOTT GARRELTS
12T	AL BUMBRY	39T BOB GIBSON
13T	RAY BURRIS	40T JIM GOTT
14T	JEFF BURROUGHS	41T DAVID GREEN
15T	BILL CAMPBELL	42T ALFREDO GRIFFIN
16T	DON CARMAN	43T OZZIE GUILLEN
17T	GARY CARTER	44T EDDIE HAAS
18T	BOBBY CASTILLO	45T TERRY HARPER
19T	BILL CAUDILL	46T TOBY HARRAH
20T	RICK CERONE	47T GREG HARRIS
21T	BRYAN CLARK	48T RON HASSEY
22T	JACK CLARK	49T RICKEY HENDERSON
23T	PAT CLEMENTS	50T STEVE HENDERSON
24T	VINCE COLEMAN	51T GEORGE HENDRICK
25T	DAVE COLLINS	52T JOE HESKETH
26T	DANNY DARWIN	53T TEDDY HIGUERA
27T	JIM DAVENPORT	54T DONNIE HILL
		55T AL HOLLAND
		56T BURT HOOTON
		57T JAY HOWELL
		58T KEN HOWELL
		59T LaMARR HOYT
		60T TIM HULETT
		61T BOB JAMES
		62T STEVE JELTZ

1985
BASEBALL
TRADED
CHECKLIST

132T

1986

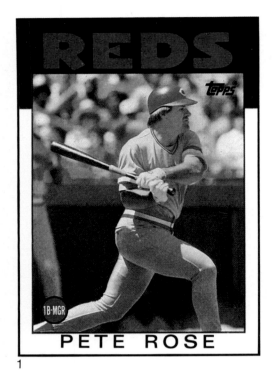

1

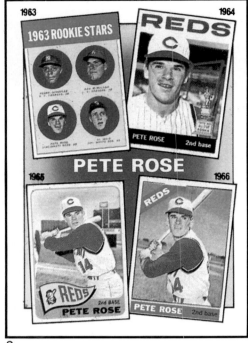

2

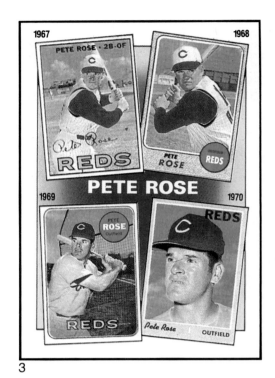

3

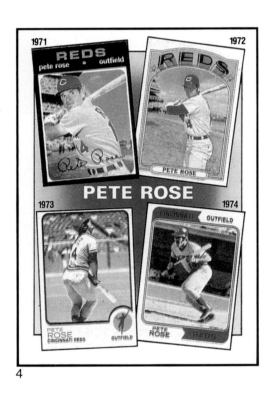

4

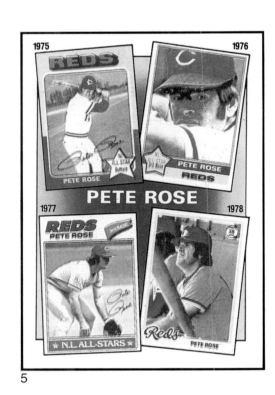

5

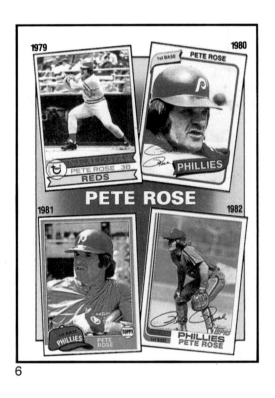

6

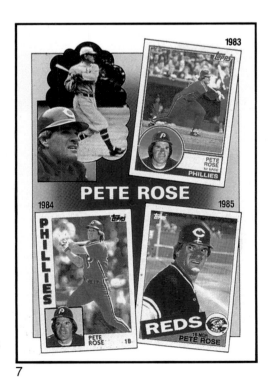

7

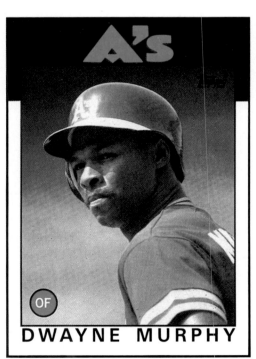

DWAYNE MURPHY

8

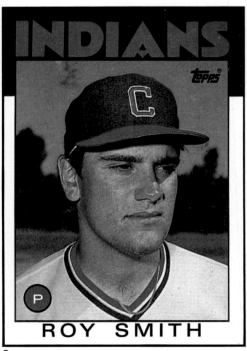

ROY SMITH

9

PADRES
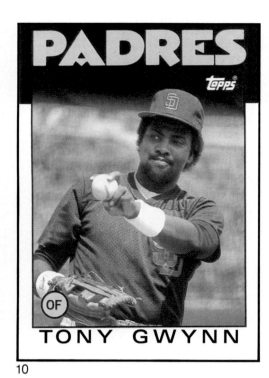
OF
TONY GWYNN
10

RED SOX
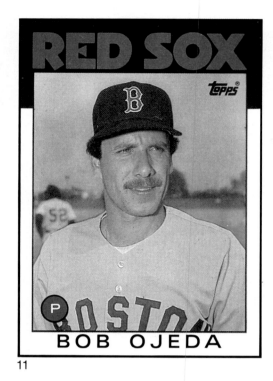
P
BOB OJEDA
11

GIANTS

SS
JOSE URIBE
12

MARINERS
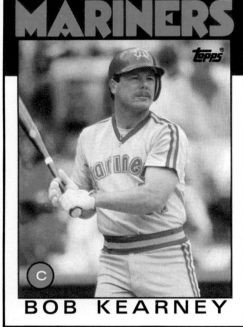
C
BOB KEARNEY
13

WHITE SOX
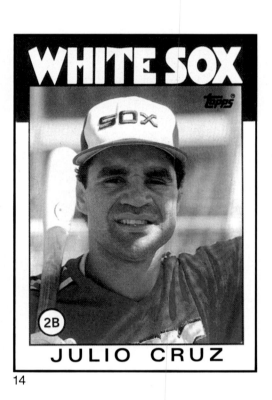
2B
JULIO CRUZ
14

YANKEES
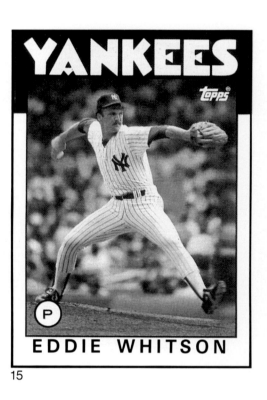
P
EDDIE WHITSON
15

PHILLIES
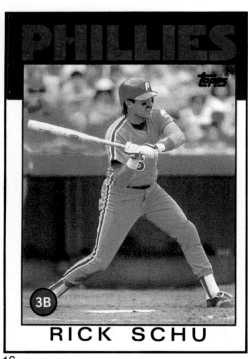
3B
RICK SCHU
16

TWINS

DH-OF
MIKE STENHOUSE
17

METS
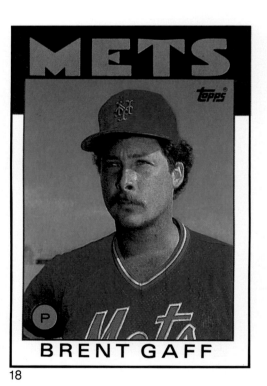
P
BRENT GAFF
18

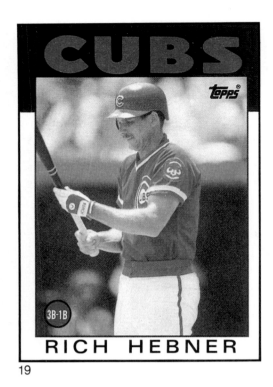

CUBS

RICH HEBNER

3B-1B

19

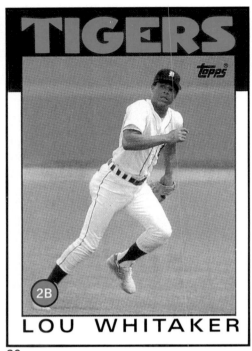

TIGERS

LOU WHITAKER

2B

20

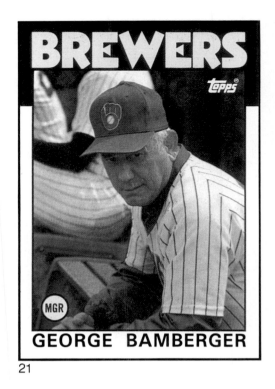

BREWERS

GEORGE BAMBERGER

MGR

21

RANGERS

DUANE WALKER

DH-OF

22

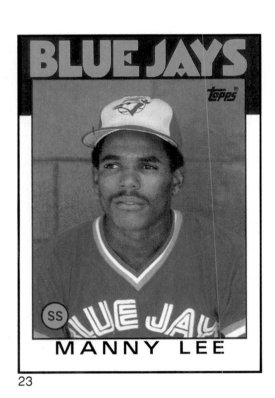

BLUE JAYS

MANNY LEE

SS

23

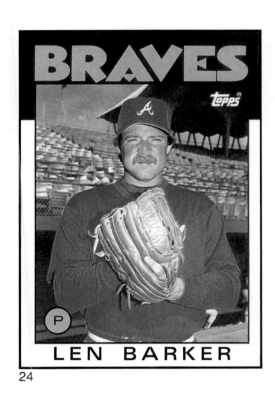

BRAVES

LEN BARKER

P

24

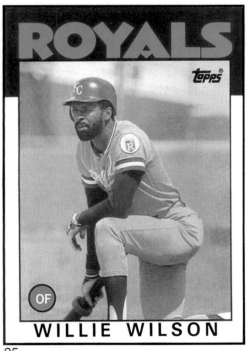

ROYALS

WILLIE WILSON

OF

25

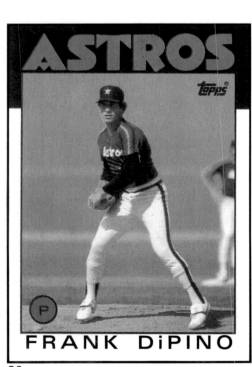

ASTROS

FRANK DiPINO

P

26

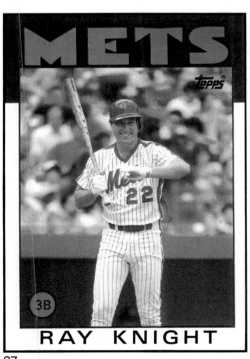

METS

RAY KNIGHT

3B

27

REDS
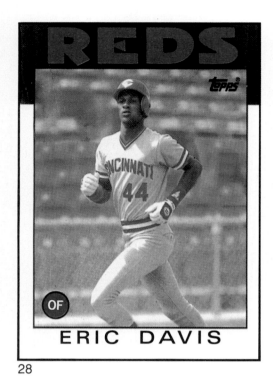
OF
ERIC DAVIS
28

A's
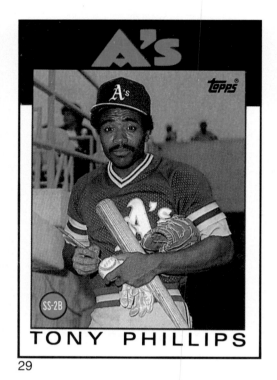
SS-2B
TONY PHILLIPS
29

ORIOLES
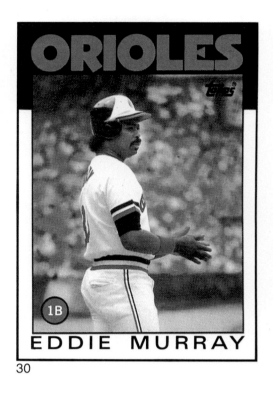
1B
EDDIE MURRAY
30

INDIANS
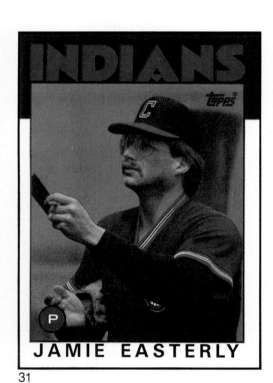
P
JAMIE EASTERLY
31

DODGERS
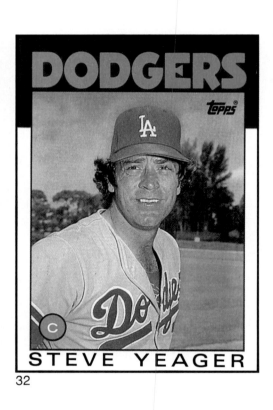
C
STEVE YEAGER
32

CARDINALS
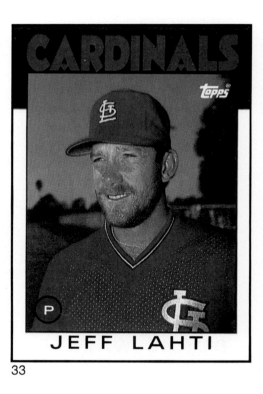
P
JEFF LAHTI
33

MARINERS
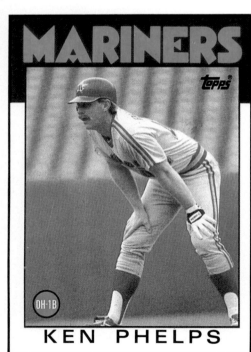
DH-1B
KEN PHELPS
34

EXPOS
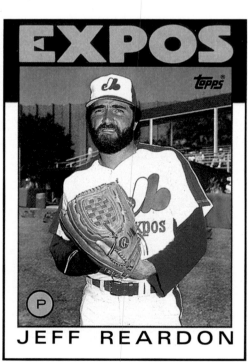
P
JEFF REARDON
35

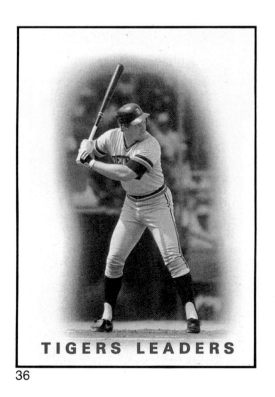
TIGERS LEADERS
36

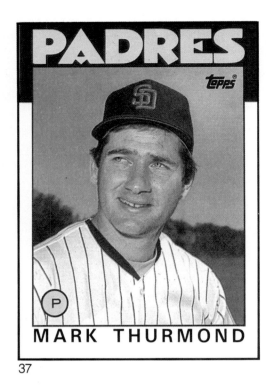

PADRES

MARK THURMOND

37

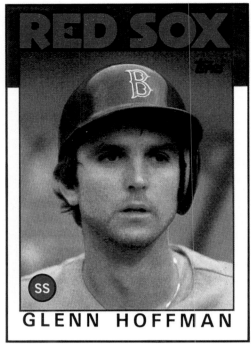

RED SOX

GLENN HOFFMAN

38

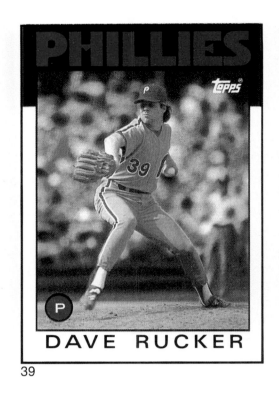

PHILLIES

DAVE RUCKER

39

YANKEES

KEN GRIFFEY

40

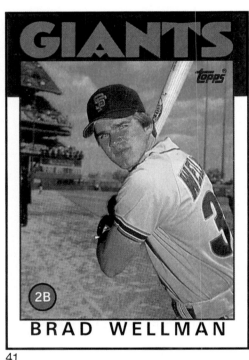

GIANTS

BRAD WELLMAN

41

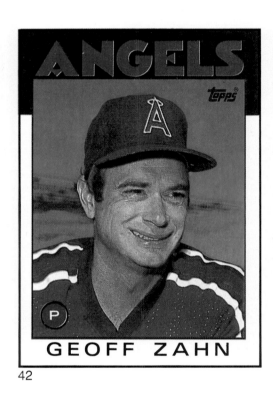

ANGELS

GEOFF ZAHN

42

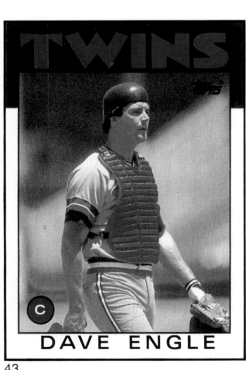

TWINS

DAVE ENGLE

43

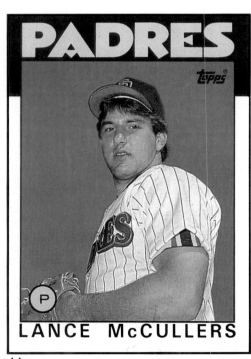

PADRES

LANCE McCULLERS

44

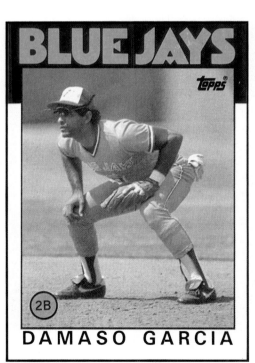

BLUE JAYS

DAMASO GARCIA

45

CUBS

OF
BILLY HATCHER
46

TIGERS
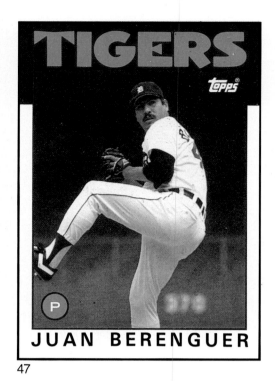
P
JUAN BERENGUER
47

PIRATES

SS-3B
BILL ALMON
48

BREWERS
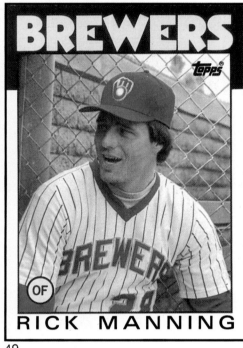
OF
RICK MANNING
49

ROYALS
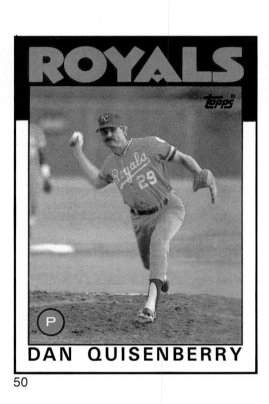
P
DAN QUISENBERRY
50

BRAVES

MGR
BOBBY WINE
51

RANGERS
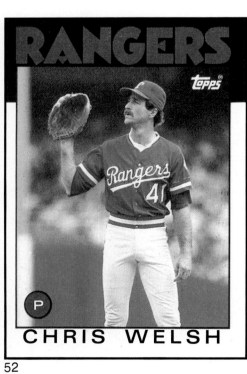
P
CHRIS WELSH
52

METS

OF
LEN DYKSTRA
53

REDS
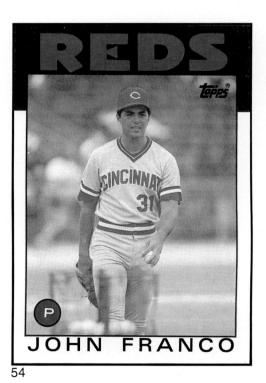
P
JOHN FRANCO
54

ORIOLES
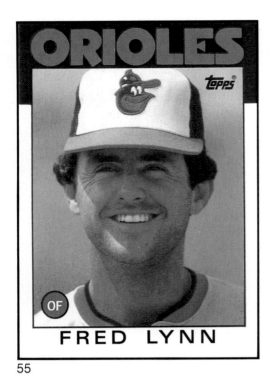
OF

FRED LYNN

55

DODGERS
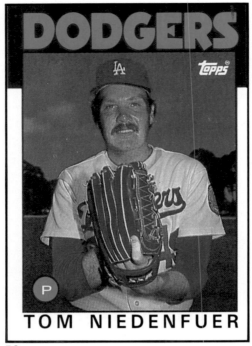
P

TOM NIEDENFUER

56

ASTROS
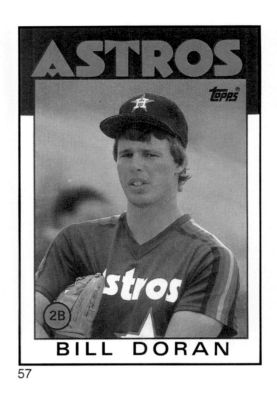
2B

BILL DORAN

57

A's
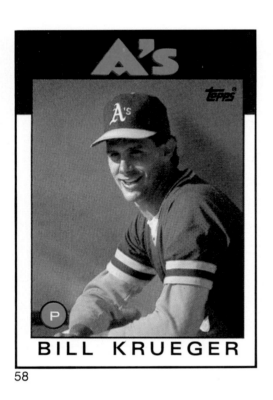
P

BILL KRUEGER

58

INDIANS
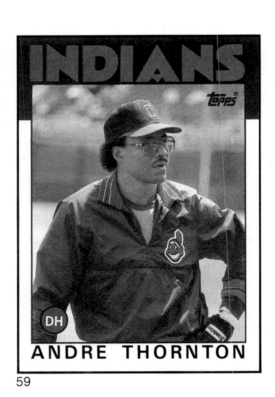
DH

ANDRE THORNTON

59

RED SOX
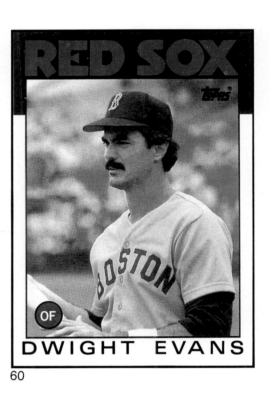
OF

DWIGHT EVANS

60

MARINERS
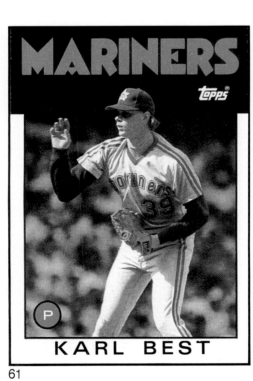
P

KARL BEST

61

ANGELS

C

BOB BOONE

62

GIANTS
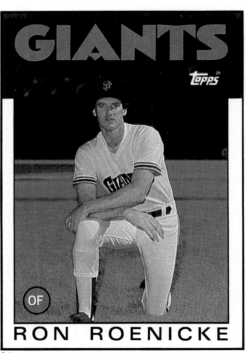
OF

RON ROENICKE

63

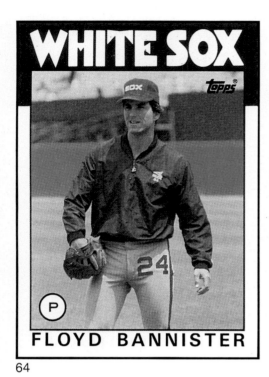

WHITE SOX

FLOYD BANNISTER

64

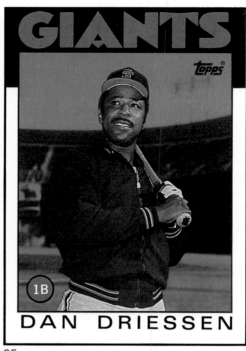

GIANTS

DAN DRIESSEN

65

CARDINALS LEADERS

66

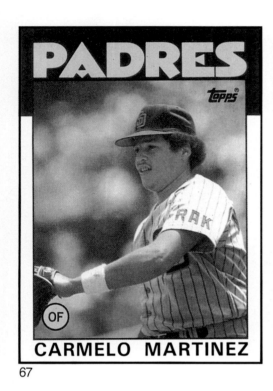

PADRES

CARMELO MARTINEZ

67

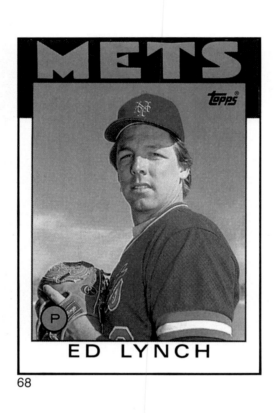

METS

ED LYNCH

68

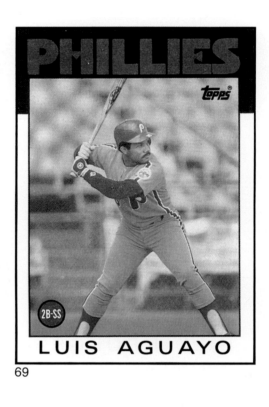

PHILLIES

LUIS AGUAYO

69

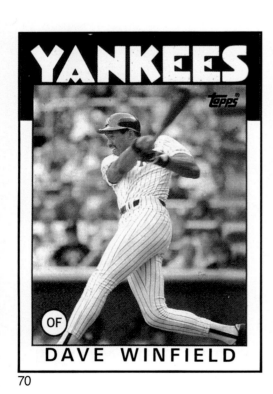

YANKEES

DAVE WINFIELD

70

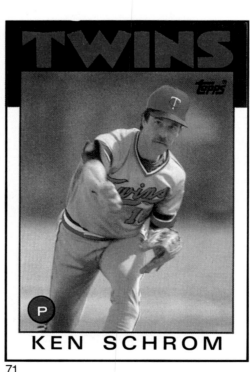

TWINS

KEN SCHROM

71

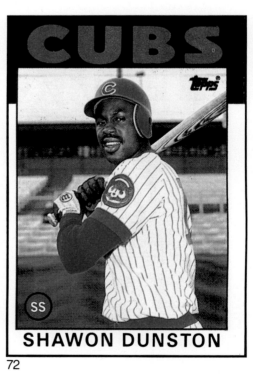

CUBS

SHAWON DUNSTON

72

TIGERS
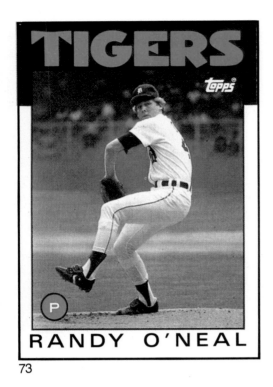
RANDY O'NEAL
73

BLUE JAYS
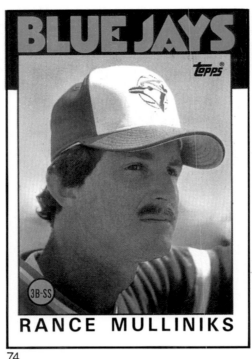
RANCE MULLINIKS
74

PIRATES
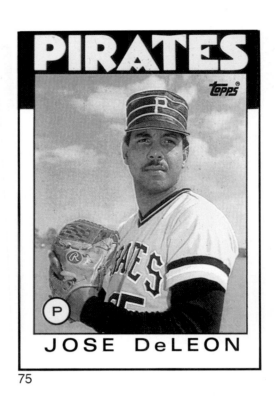
JOSE DeLEON
75

BREWERS
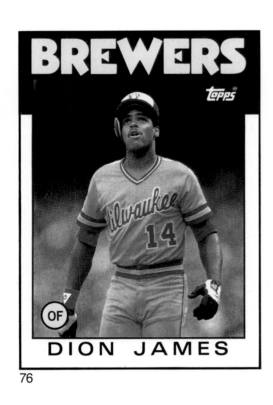
DION JAMES
76

ROYALS
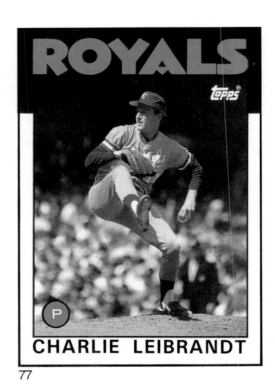
CHARLIE LEIBRANDT
77

BRAVES
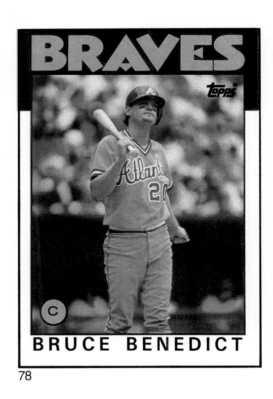
BRUCE BENEDICT
78

RANGERS
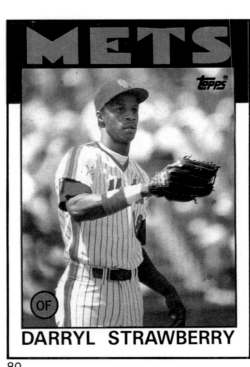
DAVE SCHMIDT
79

METS

DARRYL STRAWBERRY
80

ANGELS
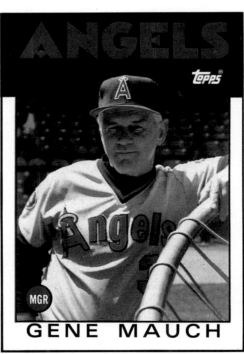
GENE MAUCH
81

ORIOLES

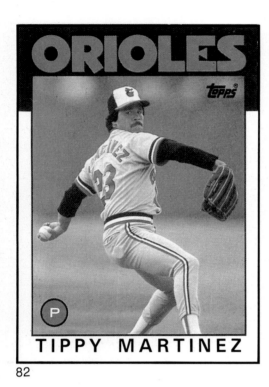

TIPPY MARTINEZ

82

ASTROS

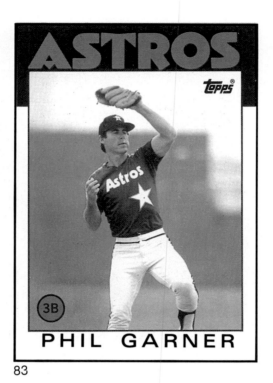

PHIL GARNER

83

A's

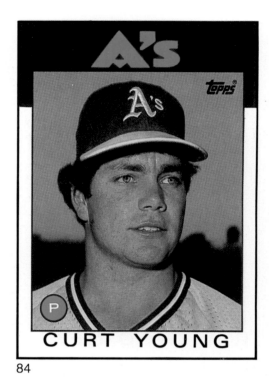

CURT YOUNG

84

REDS

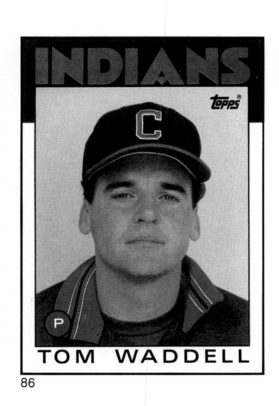

TONY PEREZ

85

INDIANS

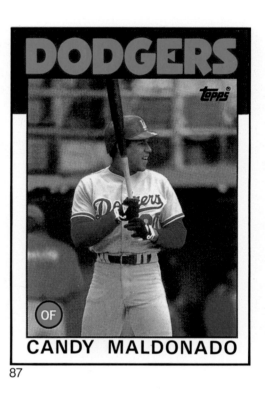

TOM WADDELL

86

DODGERS

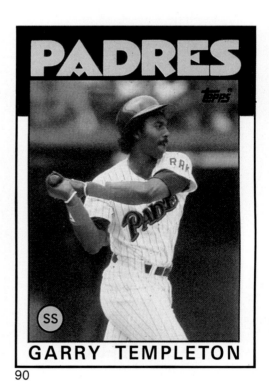

CANDY MALDONADO

87

CARDINALS

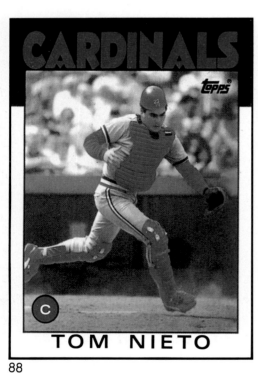

TOM NIETO

88

EXPOS

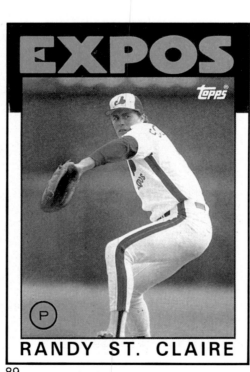

RANDY ST. CLAIRE

89

PADRES

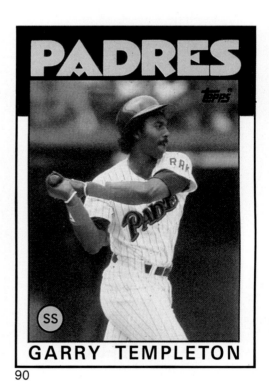

GARRY TEMPLETON

90

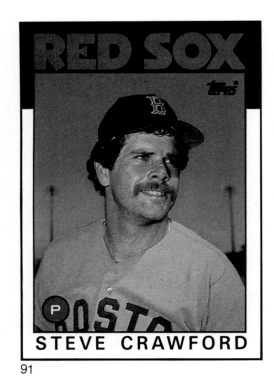
RED SOX
STEVE CRAWFORD
91

MARINERS
AL COWENS
92

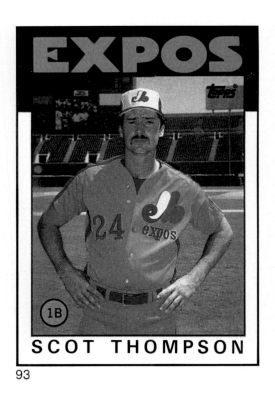
EXPOS
SCOT THOMPSON
93

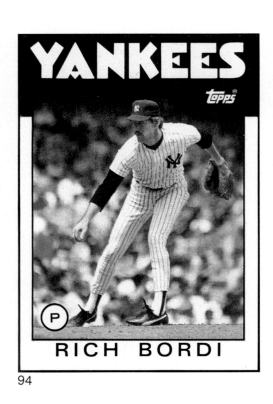
YANKEES
RICH BORDI
94

OZZIE VIRGIL
95

BLUE JAYS LEADERS
96

GARY GAETTI
97

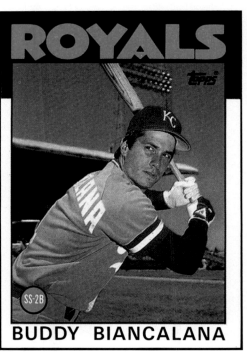
DICK RUTHVEN
98

ROYALS
BUDDY BIANCALANA
99

ASTROS
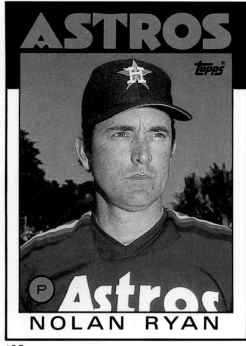
Astros
P
NOLAN RYAN
100

TIGERS

1B
DAVE BERGMAN
101

PIRATES

OF
JOE ORSULAK
102

WHITE SOX
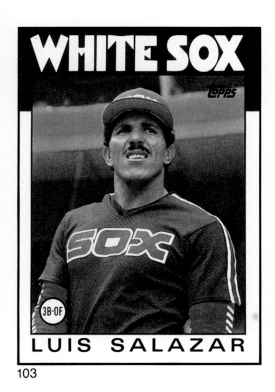
3B-OF
LUIS SALAZAR
103

METS
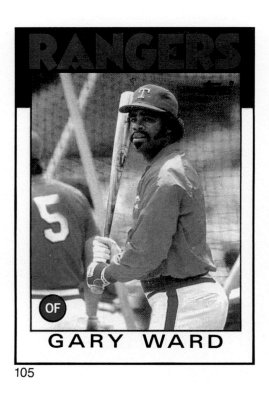
P
SID FERNANDEZ
104

RANGERS
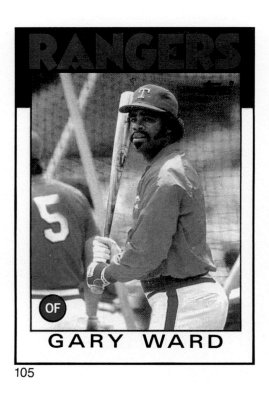
OF
GARY WARD
105

BREWERS
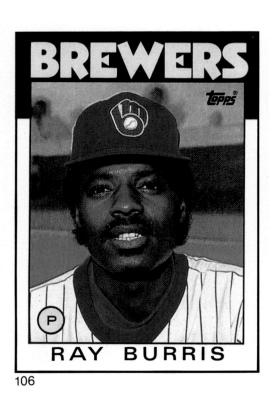
P
RAY BURRIS
106

BRAVES
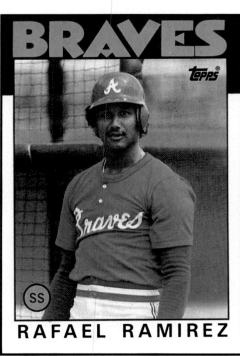
SS
RAFAEL RAMIREZ
107

REDS
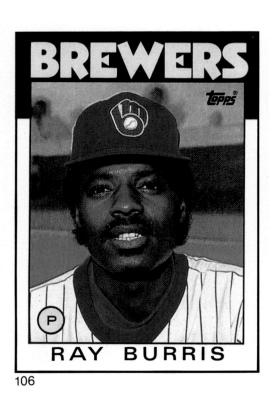
P
TED POWER
108

DODGERS
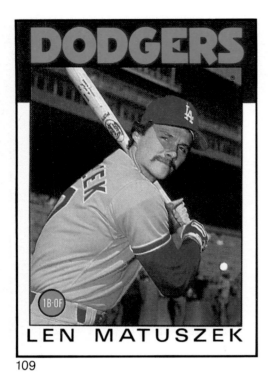
LEN MATUSZEK
109

ORIOLES
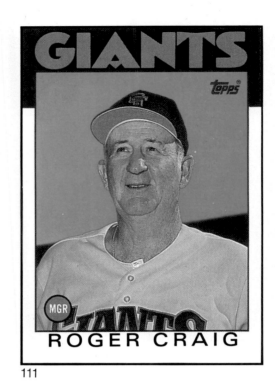
SCOTT McGREGOR
110

GIANTS
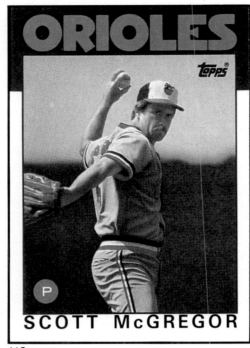
ROGER CRAIG
111

CARDINALS
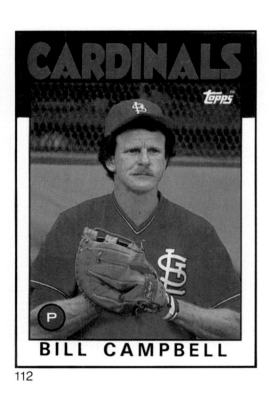
BILL CAMPBELL
112

EXPOS
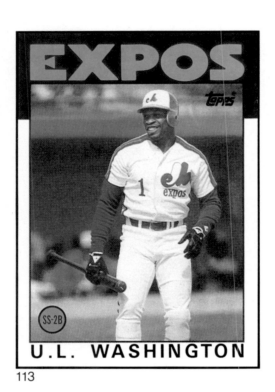
U.L. WASHINGTON
113

PIRATES
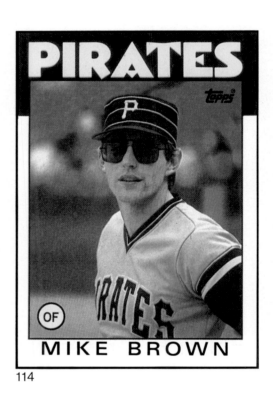
MIKE BROWN
114

A's
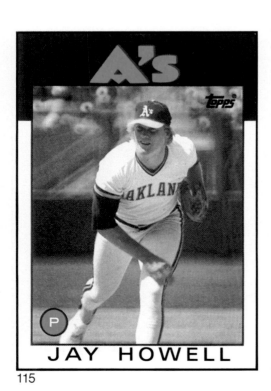
JAY HOWELL
115

INDIANS
BROOK JACOBY
116

RED SOX
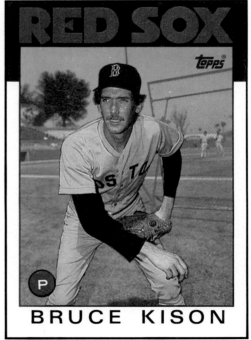
BRUCE KISON
117

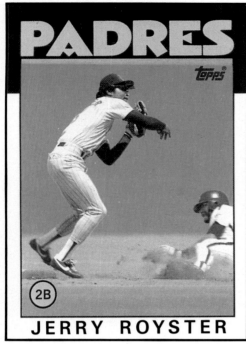

PADRES

JERRY ROYSTER

118

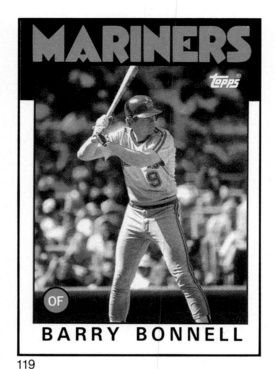

MARINERS

BARRY BONNELL

119

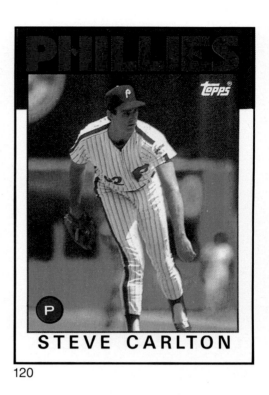

PHILLIES

STEVE CARLTON

120

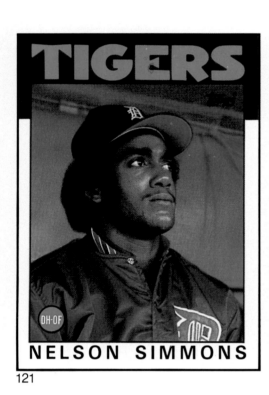

TIGERS

NELSON SIMMONS

121

TWINS

PETE FILSON

122

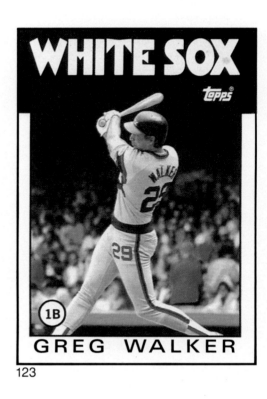

WHITE SOX

GREG WALKER

123

ANGELS

LUIS SANCHEZ

124

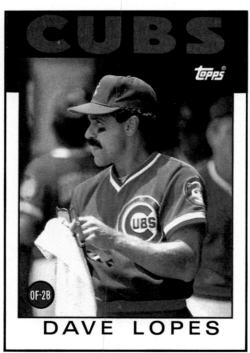

CUBS

DAVE LOPES

125

METS LEADERS

126

ANGELS

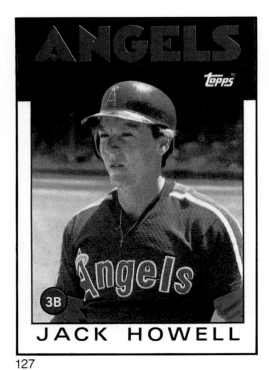

JACK HOWELL
127

ROYALS

JOHN WATHAN
128

BRAVES

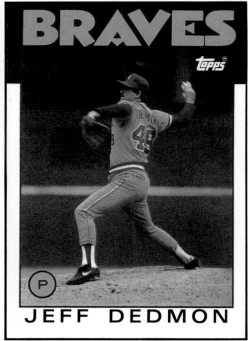

JEFF DEDMON
129

TIGERS

ALAN TRAMMELL
130

1986 BASEBALL CHECKLIST Topps CARDS 1--132

1 ☐ PETE ROSE	33 ☐ JEFF LAHTI
2 ☐ ROSE SPECIAL: '63-4-5-6	34 ☐ KEN PHELPS
3 ☐ ROSE SPECIAL: '67-8-9-70	35 ☐ JEFF REARDON
4 ☐ ROSE SPECIAL: '71-2-3-4	36 ☐ TIGERS LEADERS
5 ☐ ROSE SPECIAL: '75-6-7-8	37 ☐ MARK THURMOND
6 ☐ ROSE SPECIAL: '79-80-1-2	38 ☐ GLENN HOFFMAN
7 ☐ ROSE SPECIAL: '83-84-85	39 ☐ DAVE RUCKER
8 ☐ DWAYNE MURPHY	40 ☐ KEN GRIFFEY
9 ☐ ROY SMITH	41 ☐ BRAD WELLMAN
10 ☐ TONY GWYNN	42 ☐ GEOFF ZAHN
11 ☐ BOB OJEDA	43 ☐ DAVE ENGLE
12 ☐ JOSE URIBE	44 ☐ LANCE McCULLERS
13 ☐ BOB KEARNEY	45 ☐ DAMASO GARCIA
14 ☐ JULIO CRUZ	46 ☐ BILLY HATCHER
15 ☐ EDDIE WHITSON	47 ☐ JUAN BERENGUER
16 ☐ RICK SCHU	48 ☐ BILL ALMON
17 ☐ MIKE STENHOUSE	49 ☐ RICK MANNING
18 ☐ BRENT GAFF	50 ☐ DAN QUISENBERRY
19 ☐ RICH HEBNER	51 ☐ BOBBY WINE
20 ☐ LOU WHITAKER	52 ☐ CHRIS WELSH
21 ☐ GEORGE BAMBERGER	53 ☐ LEN DYKSTRA
22 ☐ DUANE WALKER	54 ☐ JOHN FRANCO
23 ☐ MANNY LEE	55 ☐ FRED LYNN
24 ☐ LEN BARKER	56 ☐ TOM NIEDENFUER
25 ☐ WILLIE WILSON	57 ☐ BILL DORAN
26 ☐ FRANK DIPINO	58 ☐ BILL KRUEGER
27 ☐ RAY KNIGHT	59 ☐ ANDRE THORNTON
28 ☐ ERIC DAVIS	60 ☐ DWIGHT EVANS
29 ☐ TONY PHILLIPS	61 ☐ KARL BEST
30 ☐ EDDIE MURRAY	62 ☐ BOB BOONE
31 ☐ JAMIE EASTERLY	63 ☐ RON ROENICKE
32 ☐ STEVE YEAGER	64 ☐ FLOYD BANNISTER

131

EXPOS

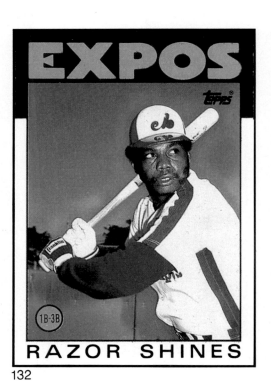

RAZOR SHINES
132

REDS

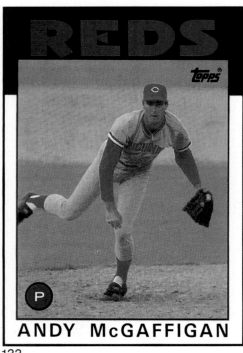

ANDY McGAFFIGAN
133

A's

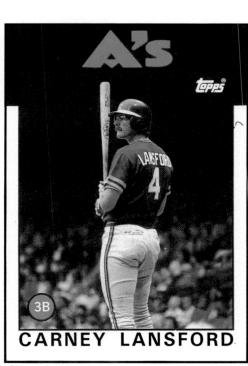

CARNEY LANSFORD
134

YANKEES

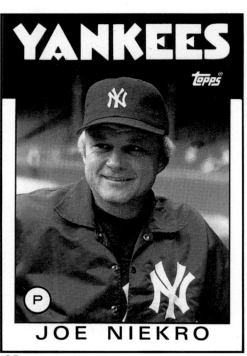

JOE NIEKRO
135

INDIANS

1B
MIKE HARGROVE
136

BREWERS
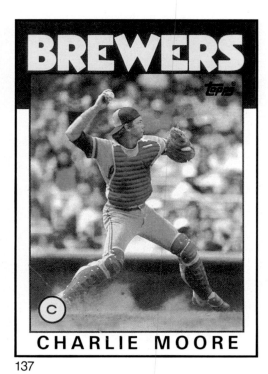
C
CHARLIE MOORE
137

GIANTS
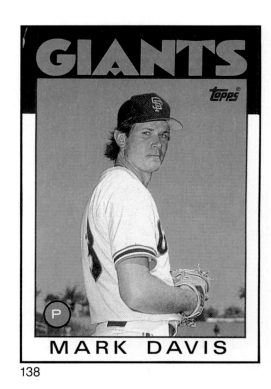
P
MARK DAVIS
138

WHITE SOX

OF
DARYL BOSTON
139

ANGELS
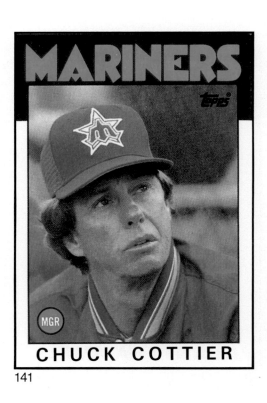
P
JOHN CANDELARIA
140

MARINERS
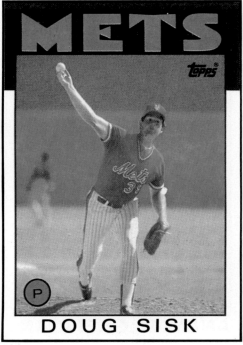
MGR
CHUCK COTTIER
141

RANGERS
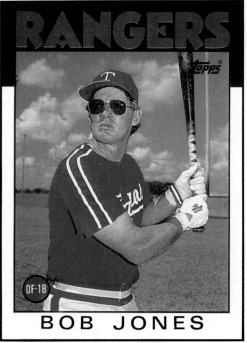
OF-1B
BOB JONES
142

REDS
C
DAVE VAN GORDER
143

METS
P
DOUG SISK
144

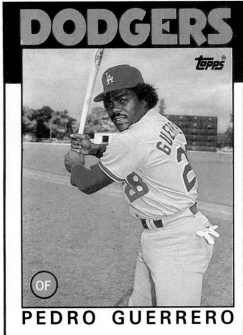

DODGERS

PEDRO GUERRERO

OF

145

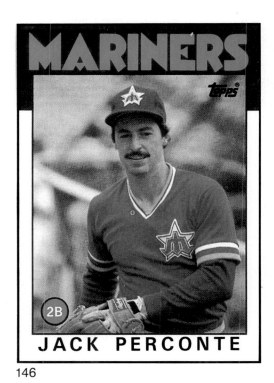

MARINERS

JACK PERCONTE

2B

146

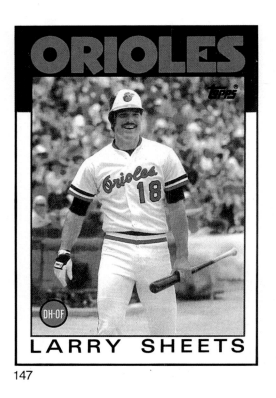

ORIOLES

LARRY SHEETS

DH-OF

147

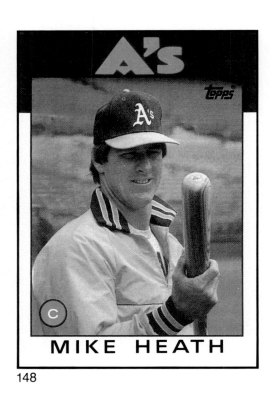

A's

MIKE HEATH

C

148

INDIANS

BRETT BUTLER

OF

149

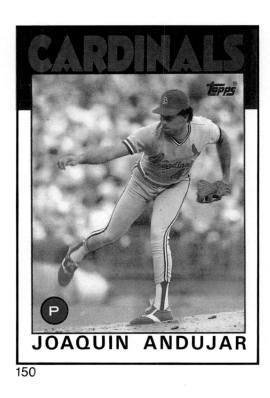

CARDINALS

JOAQUIN ANDUJAR

P

150

RED SOX

DAVE STAPLETON

1B

151

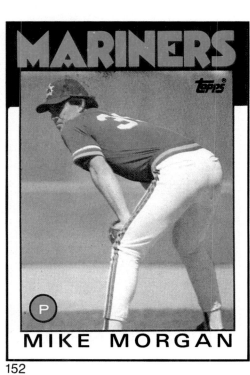

MARINERS

MIKE MORGAN

P

152

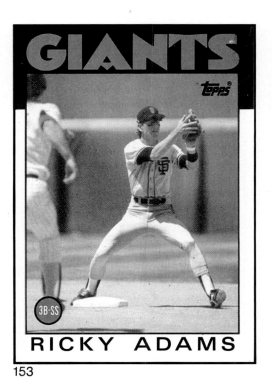

GIANTS

RICKY ADAMS

3B-SS

153

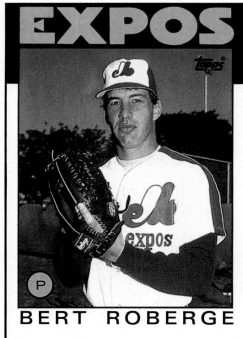

BERT ROBERGE

154

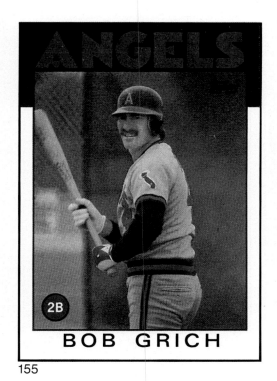

BOB GRICH

155

WHITE SOX LEADERS

156

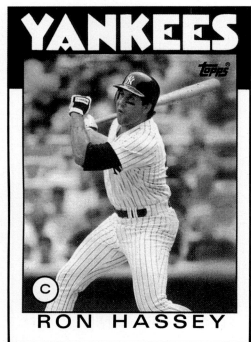

RON HASSEY

157

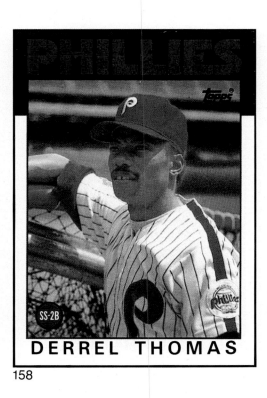

DERREL THOMAS

158

OREL HERSHISER

159

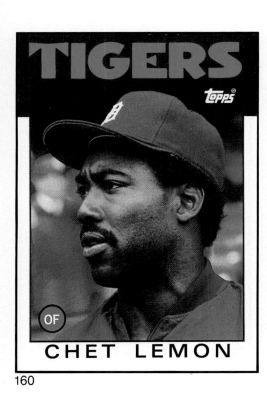

CHET LEMON

160

LEE TUNNELL

161

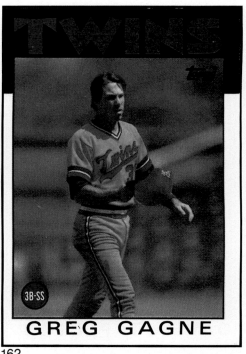

GREG GAGNE

162

BREWERS
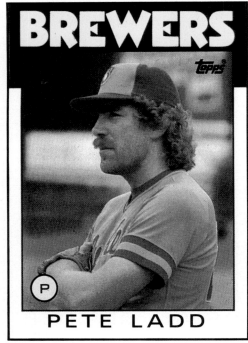
P
PETE LADD
163

ROYALS
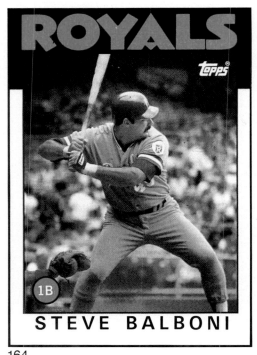
1B
STEVE BALBONI
164

A'S
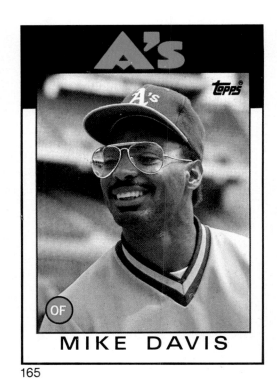
OF
MIKE DAVIS
165

ASTROS
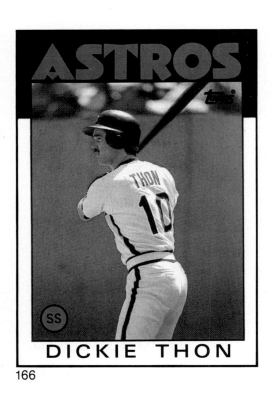
SS
DICKIE THON
166

BRAVES
ZANE SMITH
P
167

BLUE JAYS
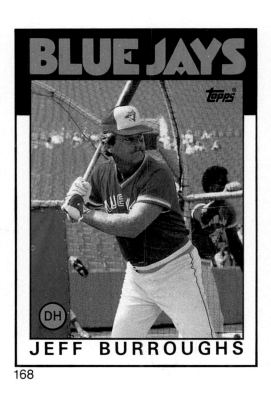
DH
JEFF BURROUGHS
168

RANGERS
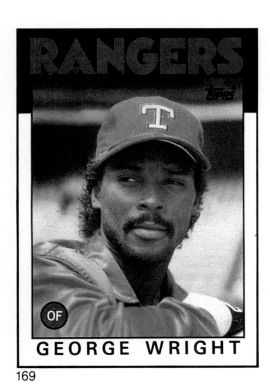
OF
GEORGE WRIGHT
169

METS
C
GARY CARTER
170

EXPOS

MGR
BOB RODGERS
171

INDIANS

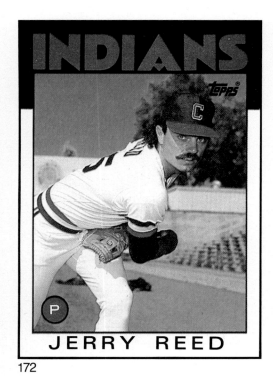

JERRY REED

172

ORIOLES

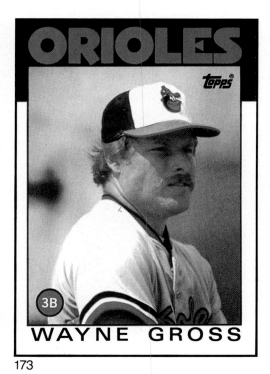

WAYNE GROSS

173

MARINERS

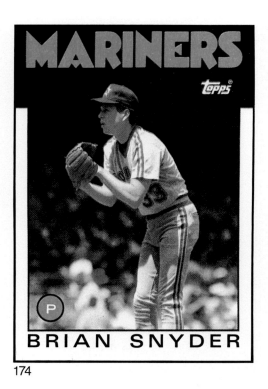

BRIAN SNYDER

174

DODGERS

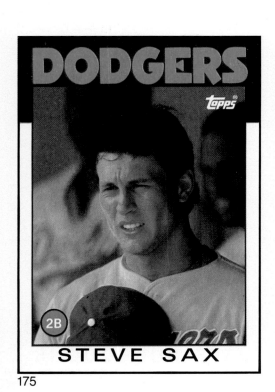

STEVE SAX

175

REDS

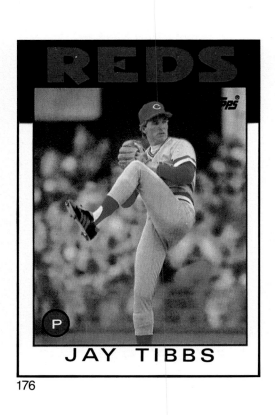

JAY TIBBS

176

GIANTS

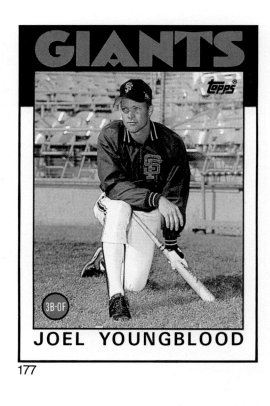

JOEL YOUNGBLOOD

177

CARDINALS

IVAN DeJESUS

178

ANGELS

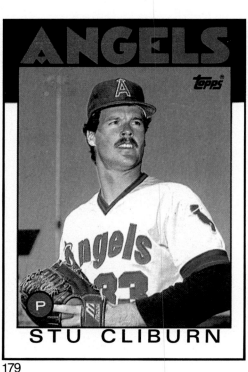

STU CLIBURN

179

YANKEES

DON MATTINGLY

180

RED SOX

AL NIPPER

181

PADRES

BOBBY BROWN

182

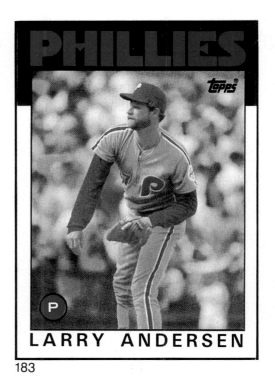

PHILLIES

LARRY ANDERSEN

183

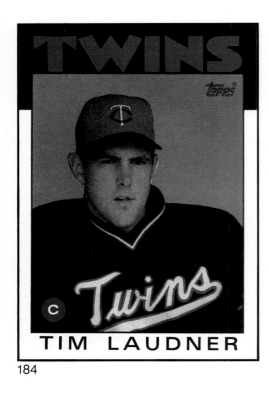

TWINS

TIM LAUDNER

184

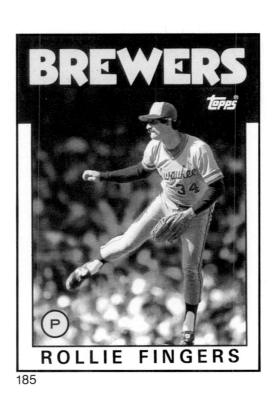

BREWERS

ROLLIE FINGERS

185

ASTROS LEADERS

186

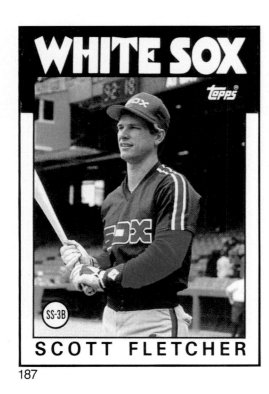

WHITE SOX

SCOTT FLETCHER

187

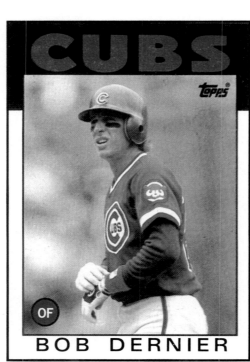

CUBS

BOB DERNIER

188

RANGERS

MIKE MASON

189

ANGELS
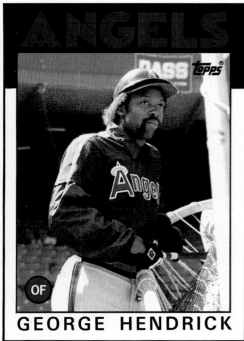
OF
GEORGE HENDRICK
190

METS
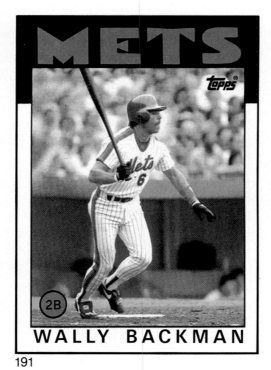
2B
WALLY BACKMAN
191

TIGERS

P
MILT WILCOX
192

ANGELS
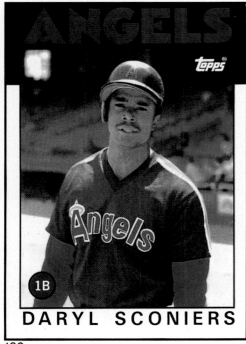
1B
DARYL SCONIERS
193

BRAVES
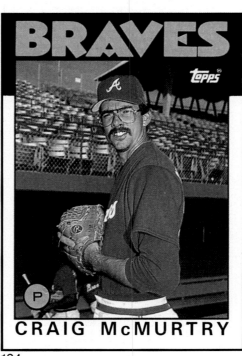
P
CRAIG McMURTRY
194

REDS
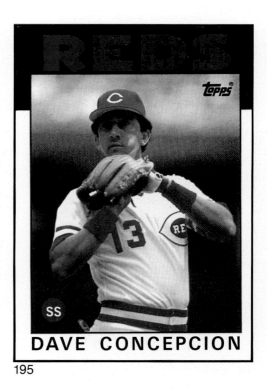
SS
DAVE CONCEPCION
195

BLUE JAYS

P
DOYLE ALEXANDER
196

DODGERS
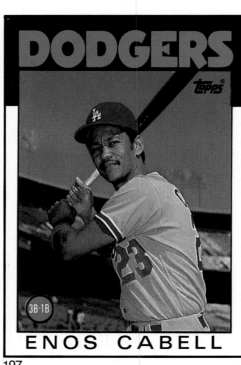
3B-1B
ENOS CABELL
197

ORIOLES
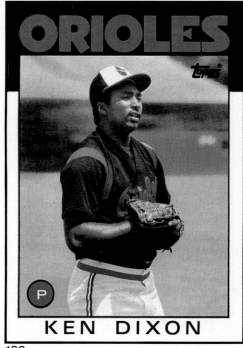
P
KEN DIXON
198

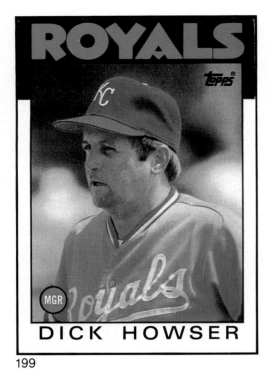

ROYALS

DICK HOWSER

199

PHILLIES

MIKE SCHMIDT

200

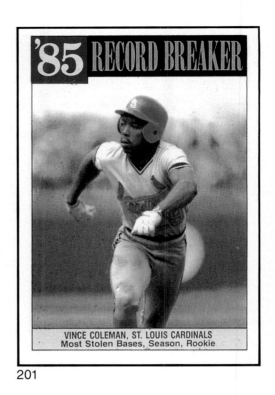

'85 RECORD BREAKER

VINCE COLEMAN, ST. LOUIS CARDINALS
Most Stolen Bases, Season, Rookie

201

'85 RECORD BREAKER

DWIGHT GOODEN, NEW YORK METS
Youngest 20-Game Winner, Modern History

202

'85 RECORD BREAKER

KEITH HERNANDEZ, NEW YORK METS
Most Game-Winning RBI, Season

203

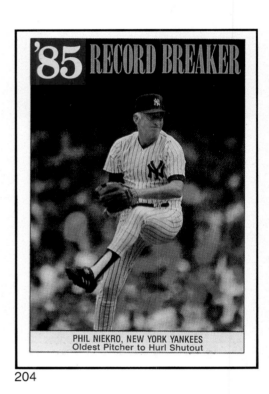

'85 RECORD BREAKER

PHIL NIEKRO, NEW YORK YANKEES
Oldest Pitcher to Hurl Shutout

204

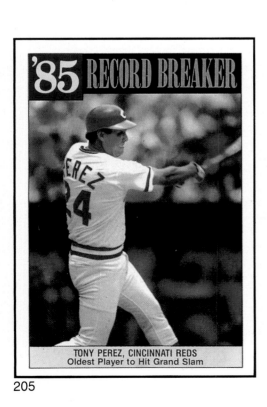

'85 RECORD BREAKER

TONY PEREZ, CINCINNATI REDS
Oldest Player to Hit Grand Slam

205

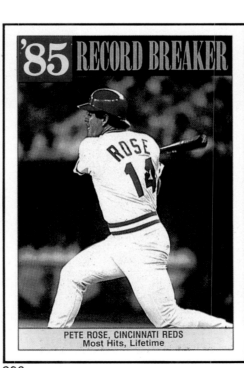

'85 RECORD BREAKER

PETE ROSE, CINCINNATI REDS
Most Hits, Lifetime

206

'85 RECORD BREAKER

FERNANDO VALENZUELA, LOS ANGELES DODGERS
Most Consecutive Innings, Start of Season, No Earned Runs

207

INDIANS

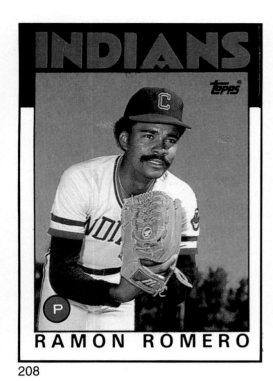

RAMON ROMERO

208

BREWERS

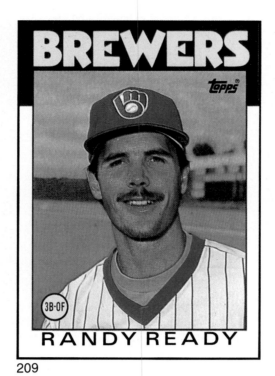

RANDY READY

209

METS

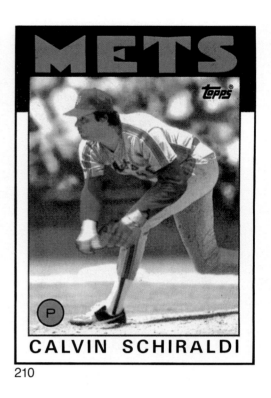

CALVIN SCHIRALDI

210

PADRES

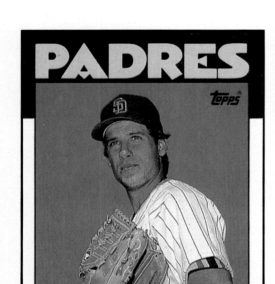

ED WOJNA

211

CUBS

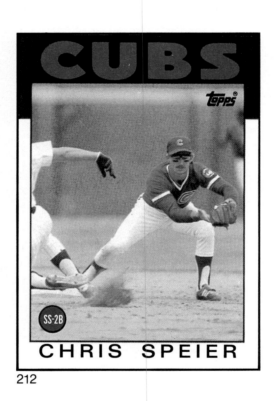

CHRIS SPEIER

212

YANKEES

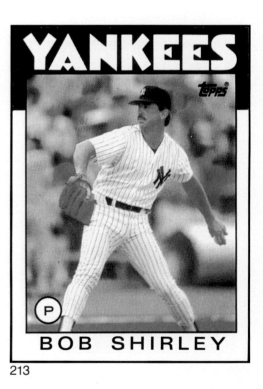

BOB SHIRLEY

213

TWINS

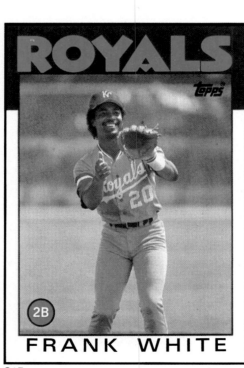

RANDY BUSH

214

ROYALS

FRANK WHITE

215

A's LEADERS

216

TIGERS

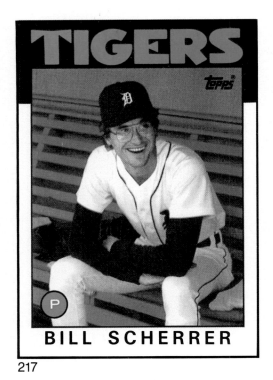

BILL SCHERRER

217

CARDINALS

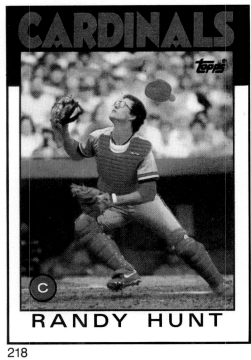

RANDY HUNT

218

BLUE JAYS

DENNIS LAMP

219

BRAVES

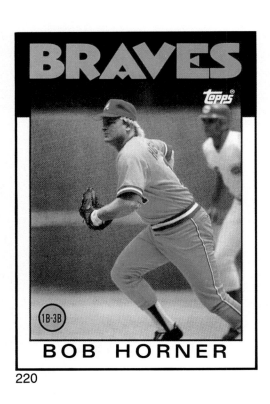

BOB HORNER

220

MARINERS

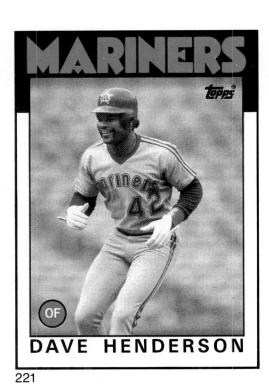

DAVE HENDERSON

221

ANGELS

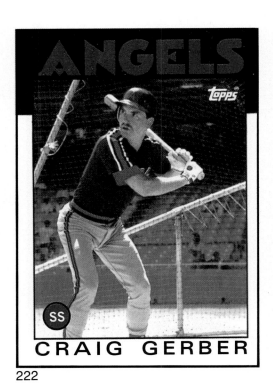

CRAIG GERBER

222

GIANTS

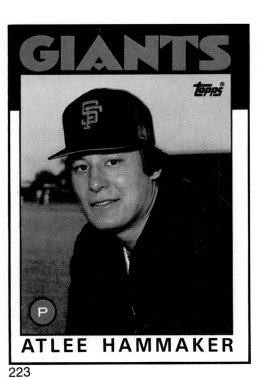

ATLEE HAMMAKER

223

CARDINALS

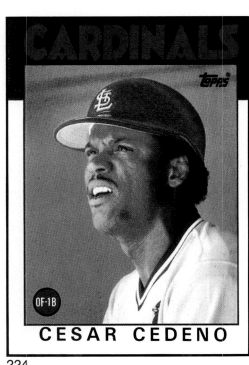

CESAR CEDENO

224

METS

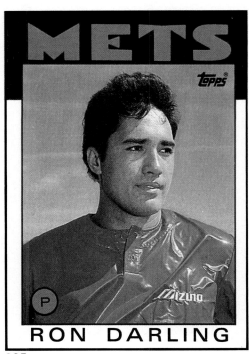

RON DARLING

225

ORIOLES
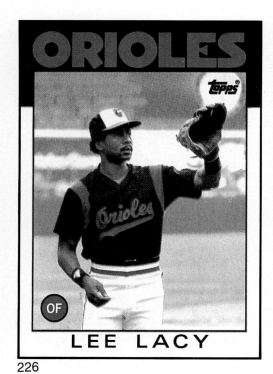
LEE LACY
OF
226

WHITE SOX
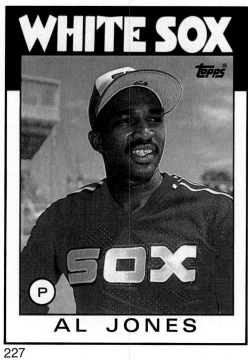
AL JONES
P
227

CARDINALS
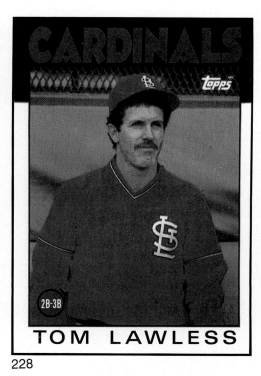
TOM LAWLESS
2B-3B
228

EXPOS
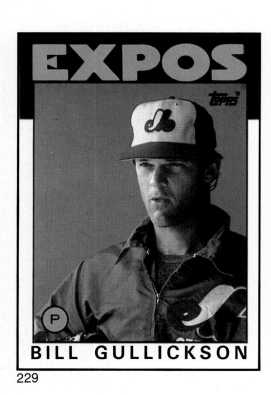
BILL GULLICKSON
P
229

PADRES
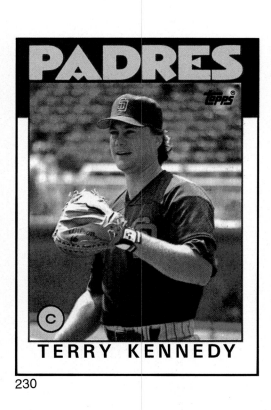
TERRY KENNEDY
C
230

CUBS
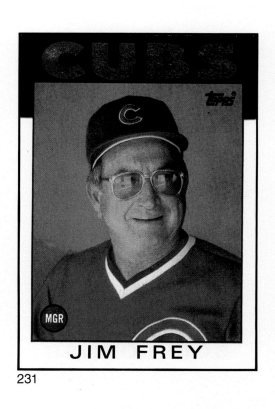
JIM FREY
MGR
231

PIRATES
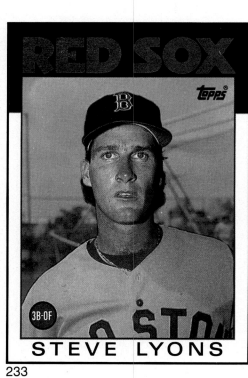
RICK RHODEN
P
232

RED SOX
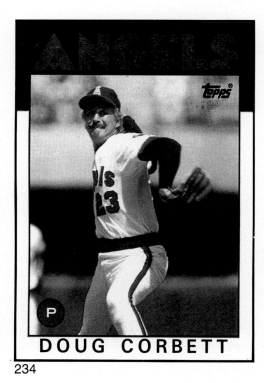
STEVE LYONS
3B-OF
233

ANGELS
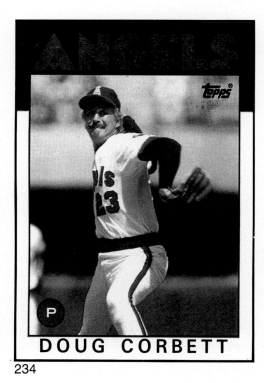
DOUG CORBETT
P
234

YANKEES
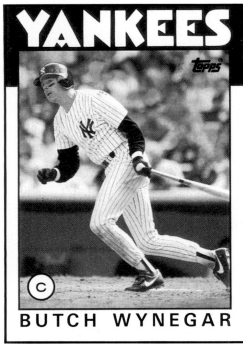
Ⓒ

BUTCH WYNEGAR

235

TWINS
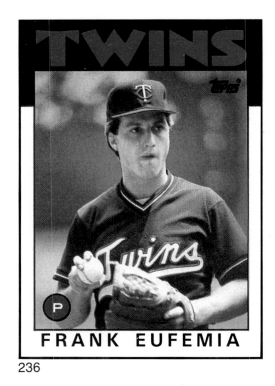
Ⓟ

FRANK EUFEMIA

236

BREWERS
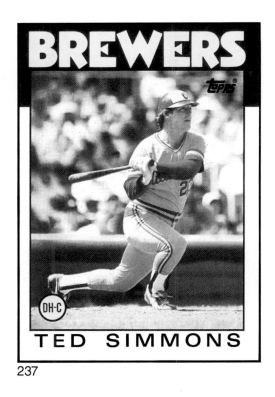
DH-C

TED SIMMONS

237

RANGERS
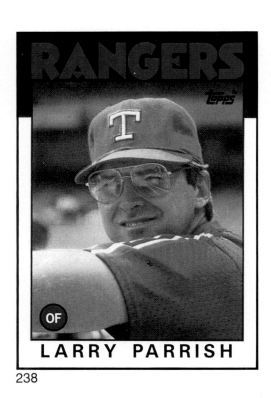
OF

LARRY PARRISH

238

WHITE SOX
Ⓒ

JOEL SKINNER

239

A's
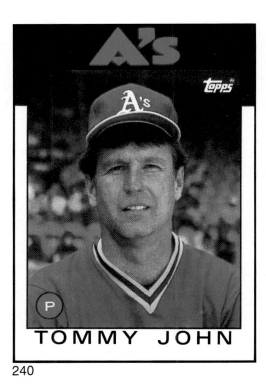
Ⓟ

TOMMY JOHN

240

BLUE JAYS
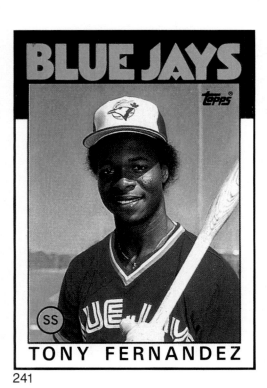
SS

TONY FERNANDEZ

241

INDIANS
Ⓟ

RICH THOMPSON

242

TIGERS
DH-OF

JOHNNY GRUBB

243

PADRES
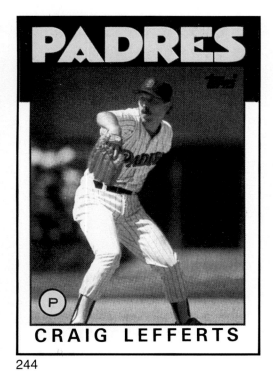
CRAIG LEFFERTS
244

ROYALS

JIM SUNDBERG
245

PHILLIES LEADERS
246

BRAVES
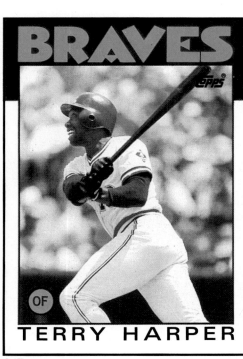
TERRY HARPER
247

MARINERS
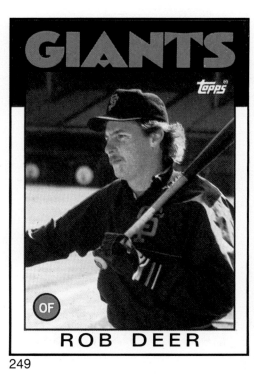
SPIKE OWEN
248

GIANTS

ROB DEER
249

METS

DWIGHT GOODEN
250

ORIOLES
RICH DAUER
251

DODGERS
BOBBY CASTILLO
252

REDS
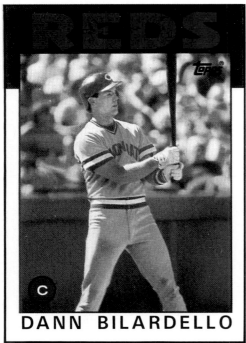
C
DANN BILARDELLO
253

WHITE SOX
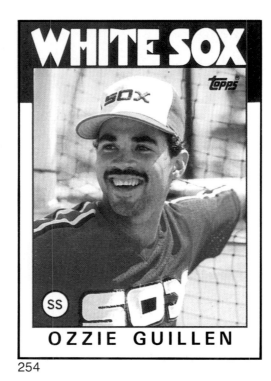
SS
OZZIE GUILLEN
254

RED SOX
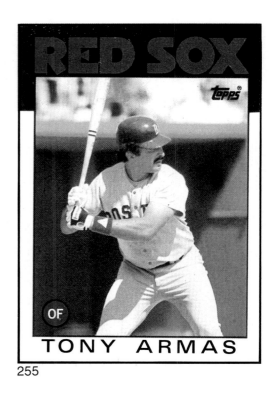
OF
TONY ARMAS
255

CARDINALS
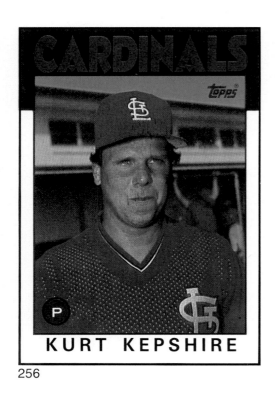
P
KURT KEPSHIRE
256

ANGELS
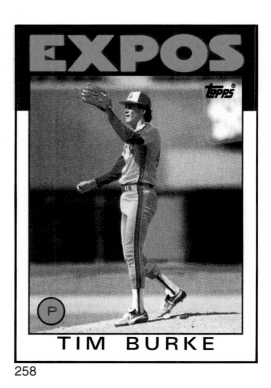
3B
DOUG DeCINCES
257

EXPOS
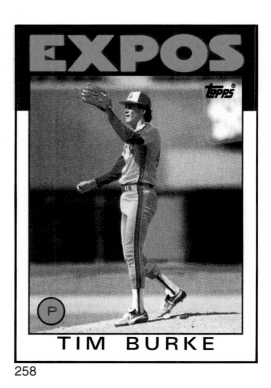
P
TIM BURKE
258

YANKEES

DH-OF
DAN PASQUA
259

PIRATES
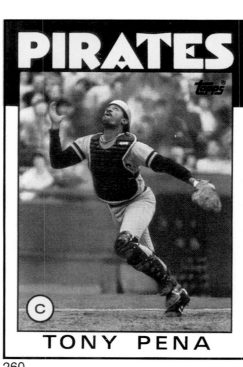
C
TONY PENA
260

RANGERS
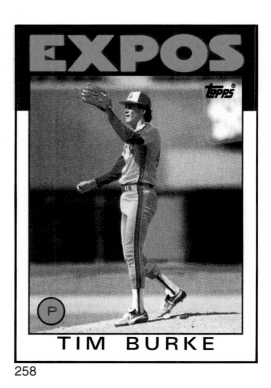
MGR
BOBBY VALENTINE
261

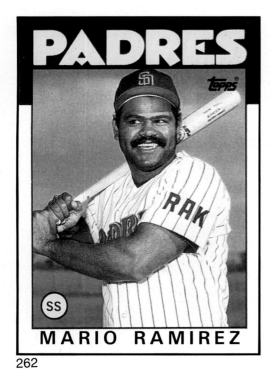

PADRES

MARIO RAMIREZ

262

263

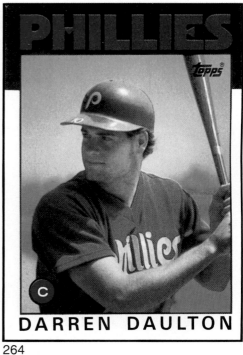

PHILLIES

DARREN DAULTON

264

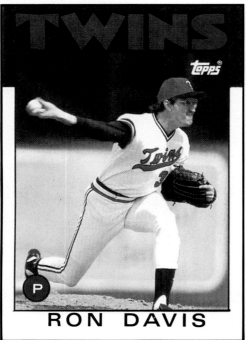

TWINS

RON DAVIS

265

CUBS

KEITH MORELAND

266

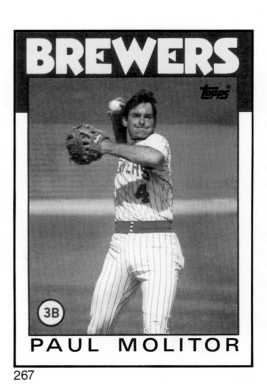

BREWERS

PAUL MOLITOR

267

ASTROS

MIKE SCOTT

268

ROYALS

DANE IORG

269

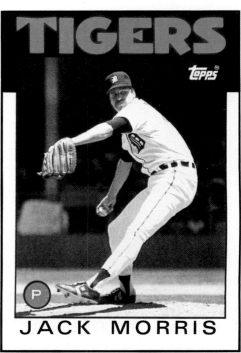

TIGERS

JACK MORRIS

270

DAVE COLLINS

271

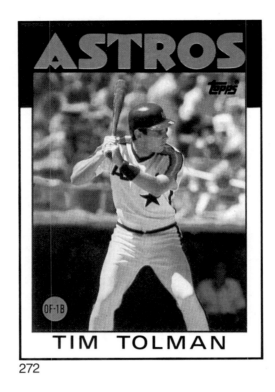

TIM TOLMAN

272

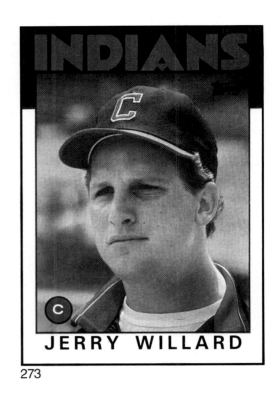

JERRY WILLARD

273

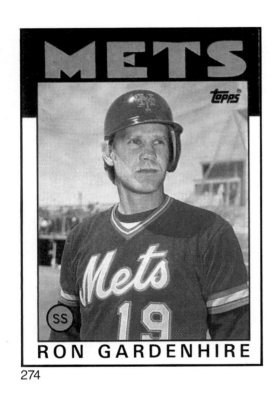

RON GARDENHIRE

274

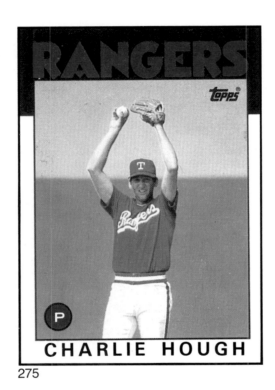

CHARLIE HOUGH

275

YANKEES LEADERS

276

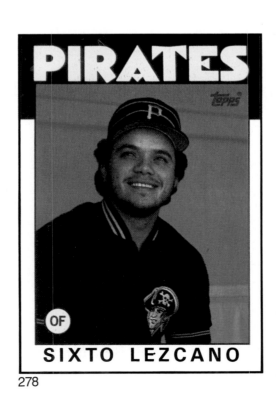

JAIME COCANOWER

277

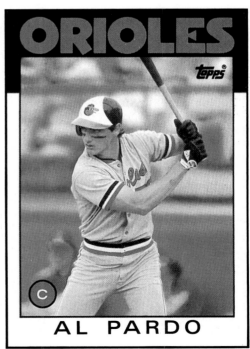

SIXTO LEZCANO

278

ORIOLES

AL PARDO

279

EXPOS
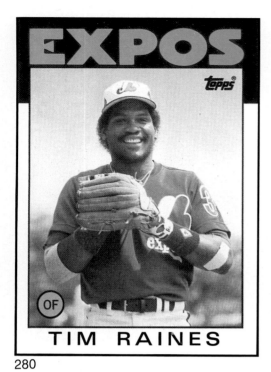
TIM RAINES OF
280

A's
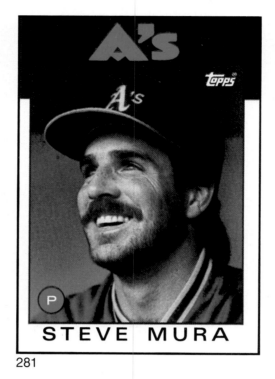
STEVE MURA P
281

ASTROS
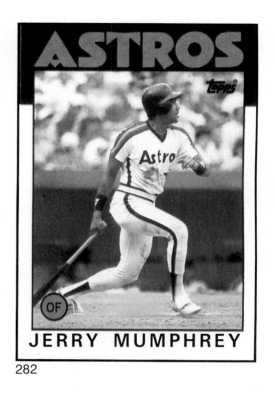
JERRY MUMPHREY OF
282

INDIANS

MIKE FISCHLIN SS-2B
283

CUBS
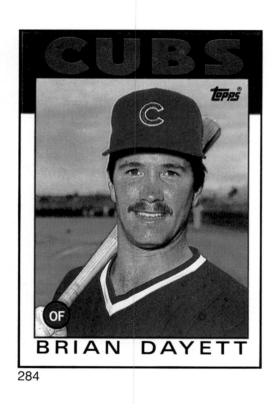
BRIAN DAYETT OF
284

REDS

BUDDY BELL 3B
285

PADRES
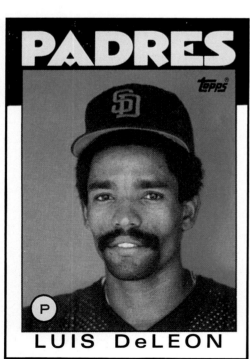
LUIS DeLEON P
286

METS

JOHN CHRISTENSEN OF
287

ORIOLES
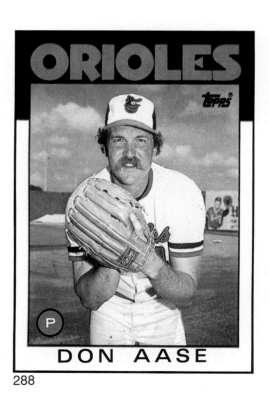
DON AASE P
288

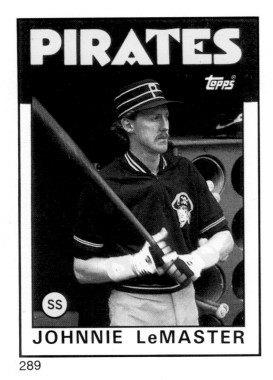

PIRATES

JOHNNIE LeMASTER

289

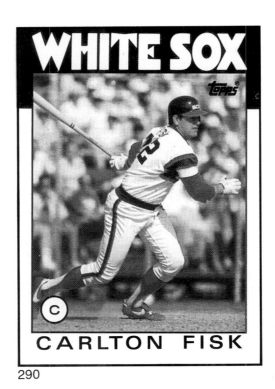

WHITE SOX

CARLTON FISK

290

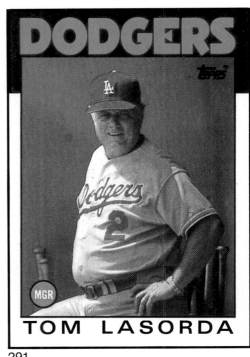

DODGERS

TOM LASORDA

291

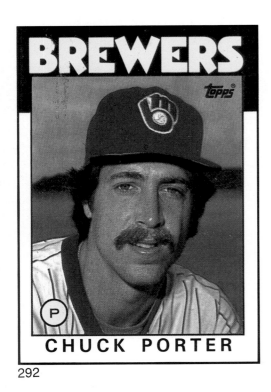

BREWERS

CHUCK PORTER

292

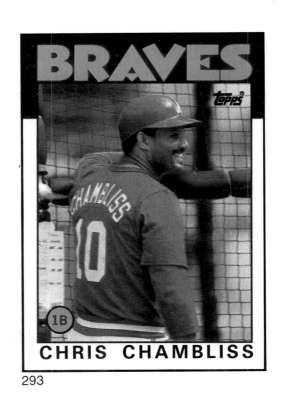

BRAVES

CHRIS CHAMBLISS

293

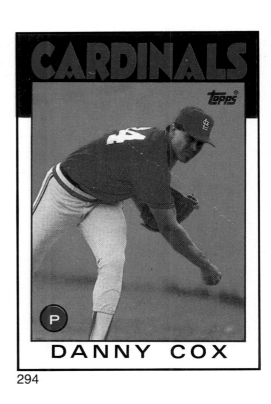

CARDINALS

DANNY COX

294

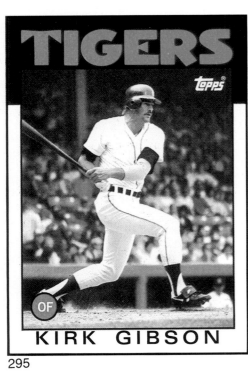

TIGERS

KIRK GIBSON

295

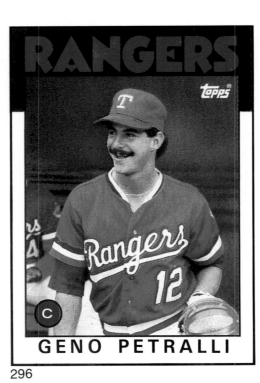

RANGERS

GENO PETRALLI

296

RED SOX

TIM LOLLAR

297

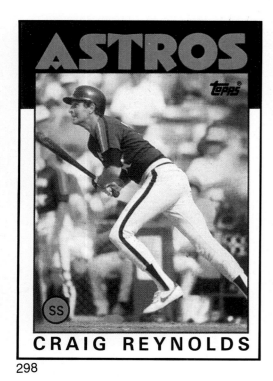

ASTROS

Topps

SS

CRAIG REYNOLDS

298

EXPOS

Topps

P

BRYN SMITH

299

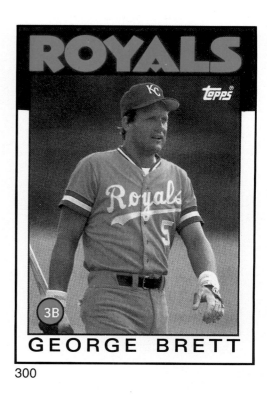

ROYALS

Topps

3B

GEORGE BRETT

300

YANKEES

Topps

P

DENNIS RASMUSSEN

301

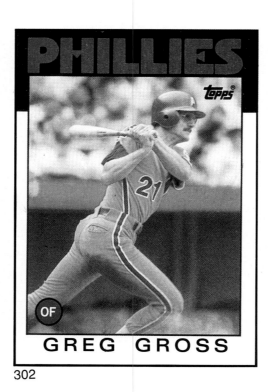

PHILLIES

Topps

OF

GREG GROSS

302

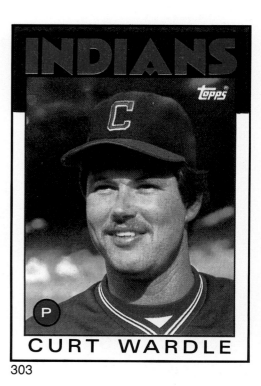

INDIANS

Topps

P

CURT WARDLE

303

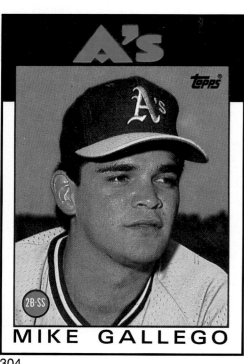

A's

Topps

2B-SS

MIKE GALLEGO

304

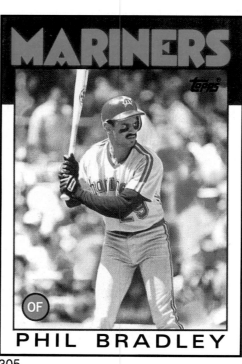

MARINERS

Topps

OF

PHIL BRADLEY

305

PADRES LEADERS

306

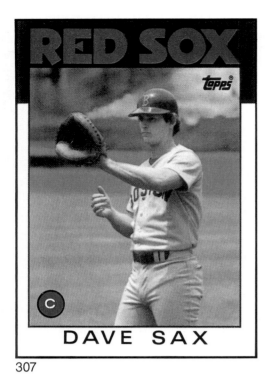

RED SOX

DAVE SAX

307

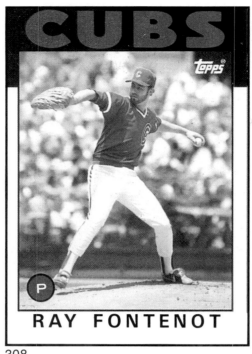

CUBS

RAY FONTENOT

308

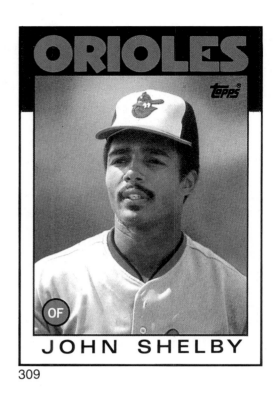

ORIOLES

JOHN SHELBY

309

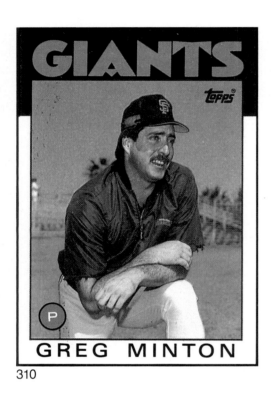

GIANTS

GREG MINTON

310

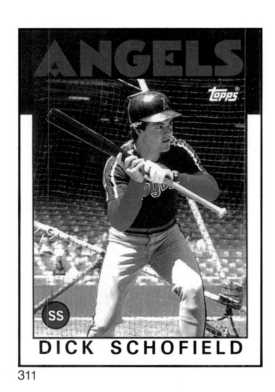

ANGELS

DICK SCHOFIELD

311

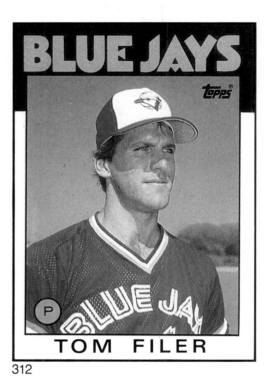

BLUE JAYS

TOM FILER

312

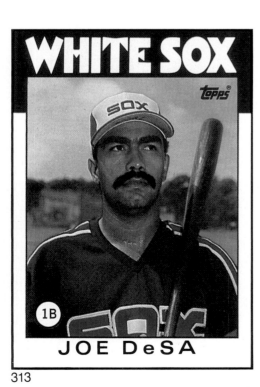

WHITE SOX

JOE DeSA

313

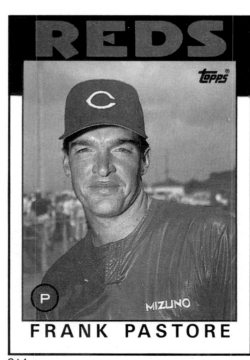

REDS

FRANK PASTORE

314

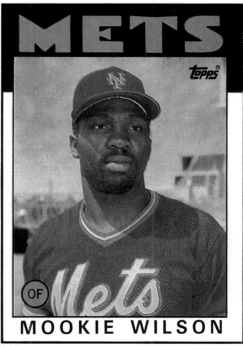

METS

MOOKIE WILSON

315

PIRATES

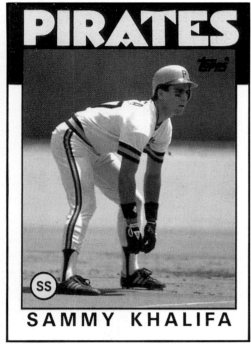

SAMMY KHALIFA

316

BREWERS

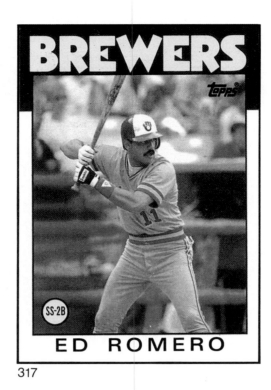

ED ROMERO

317

DODGERS

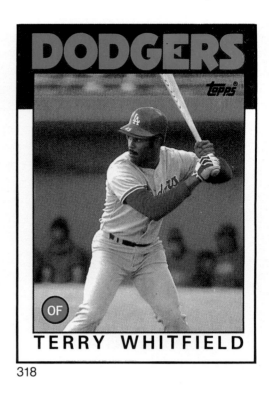

TERRY WHITFIELD

318

BRAVES

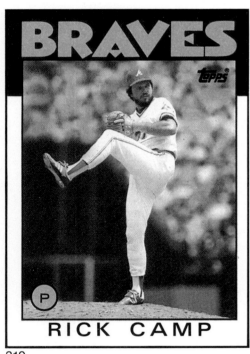

RICK CAMP

319

RED SOX

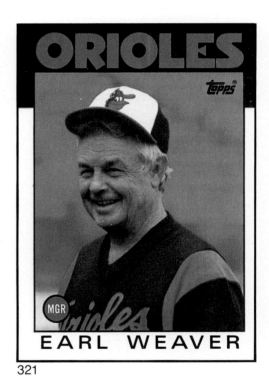

JIM RICE

320

ORIOLES

EARL WEAVER

321

CARDINALS

BOB FORSCH

322

PADRES

JERRY DAVIS

323

EXPOS

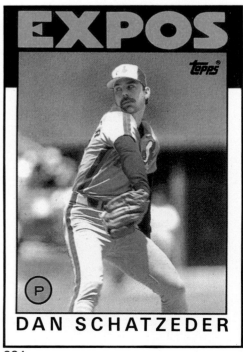

DAN SCHATZEDER

324

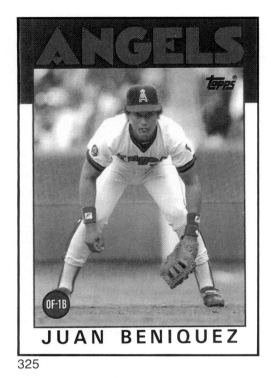

JUAN BENIQUEZ

325

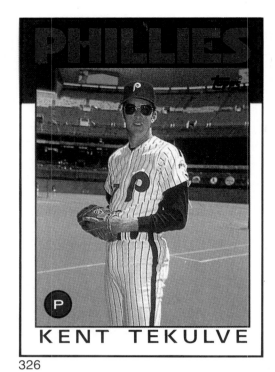

KENT TEKULVE

326

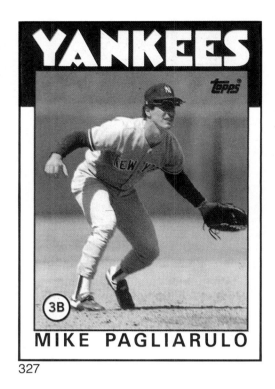

MIKE PAGLIARULO

327

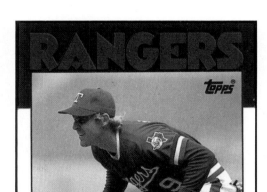

PETE O'BRIEN

328

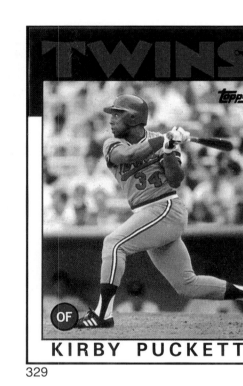

KIRBY PUCKETT

329

RICK SUTCLIFFE

330

ALAN ASHBY

331

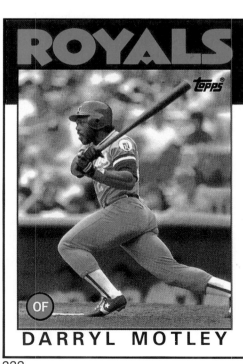

DARRYL MOTLEY

332

TOM HENKE

333

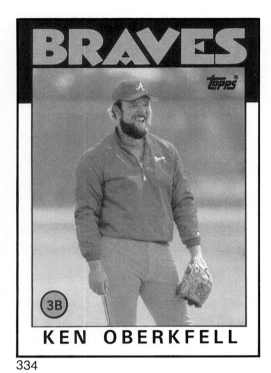

KEN OBERKFELL

334

DON SUTTON

335

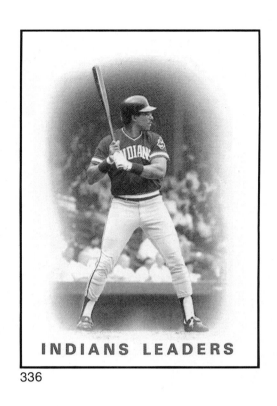

INDIANS LEADERS

336

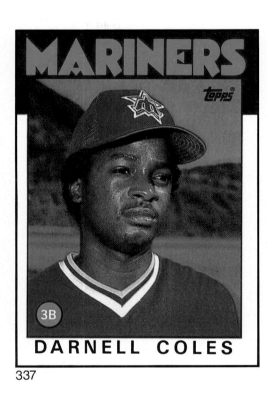

DARNELL COLES

337

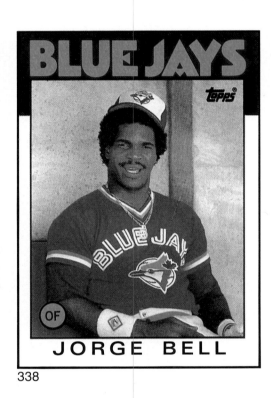

JORGE BELL

338

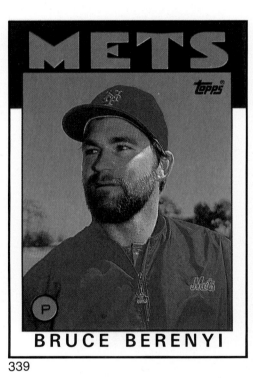

BRUCE BERENYI

339

CAL RIPKEN

340

FRANK WILLIAMS

341

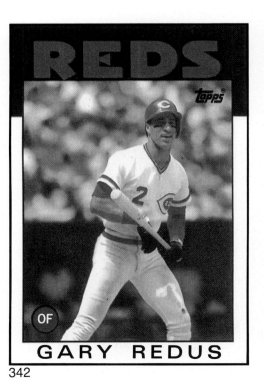

GARY REDUS

342

DODGERS
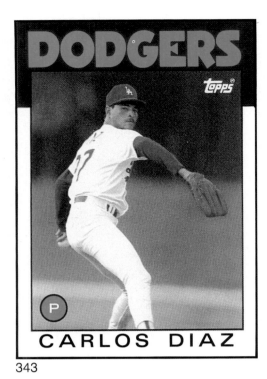
CARLOS DIAZ
343

EXPOS
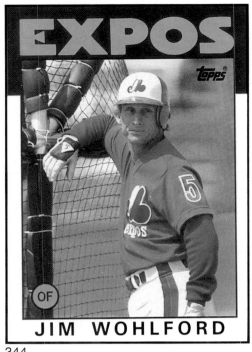
JIM WOHLFORD
344

ANGELS
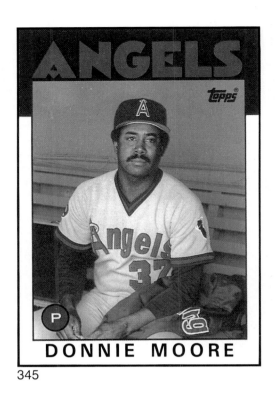
DONNIE MOORE
345

WHITE SOX
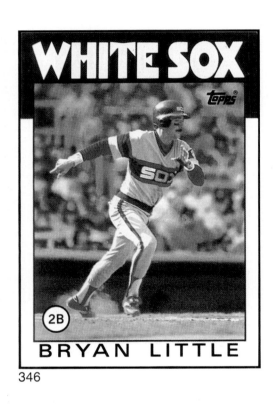
BRYAN LITTLE
346

BREWERS
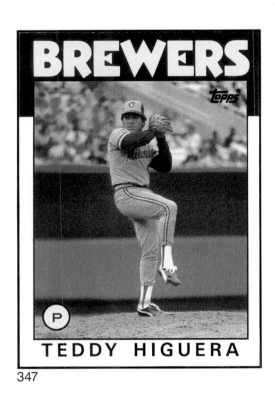
TEDDY HIGUERA
347

BLUE JAYS
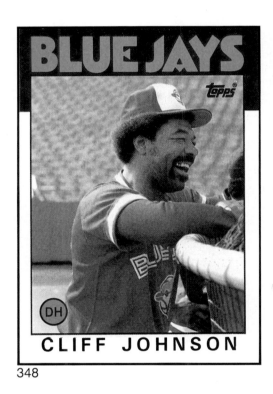
CLIFF JOHNSON
348

RED SOX
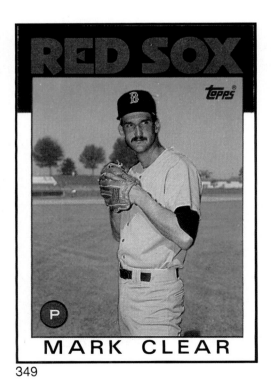
MARK CLEAR
349

CARDINALS

JACK CLARK
350

PIRATES
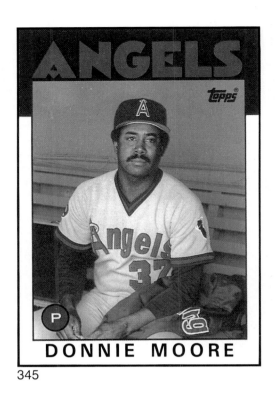
CHUCK TANNER
351

ASTROS

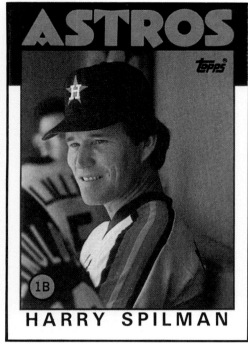

HARRY SPILMAN
352

A's

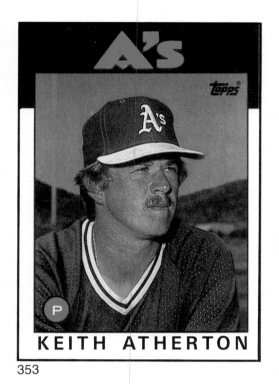

KEITH ATHERTON
353

INDIANS

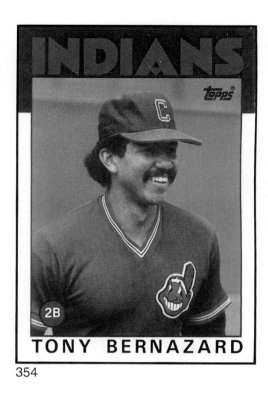

TONY BERNAZARD
354

CUBS

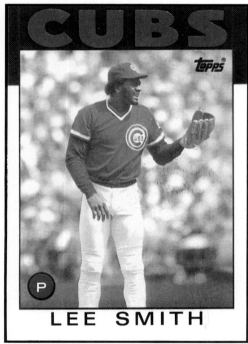

LEE SMITH
355

TWINS

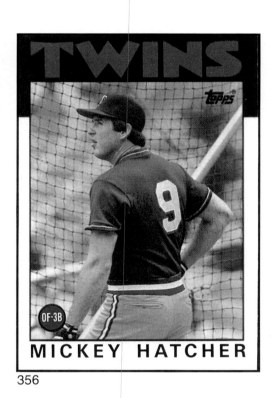

MICKEY HATCHER
356

MARINERS

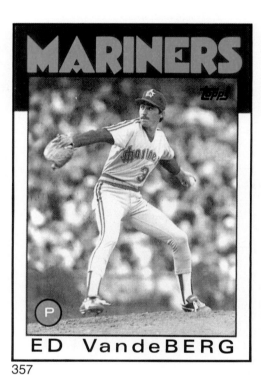

ED VandeBERG
357

ORIOLES

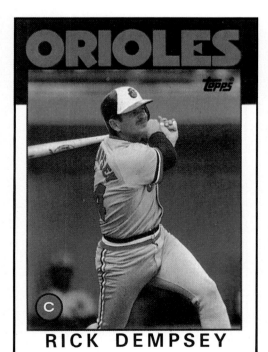

RICK DEMPSEY
358

ROYALS

MIKE LaCOSS
359

BLUE JAYS

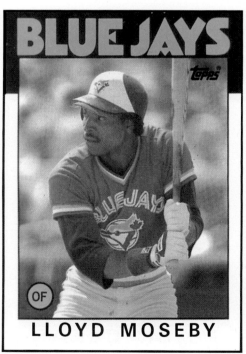

LLOYD MOSEBY
360

PHILLIES

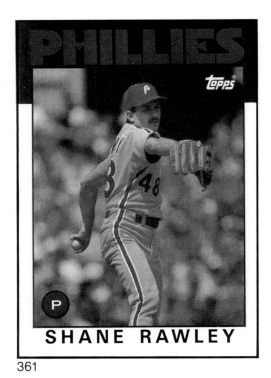

Ⓟ

SHANE RAWLEY

361

METS

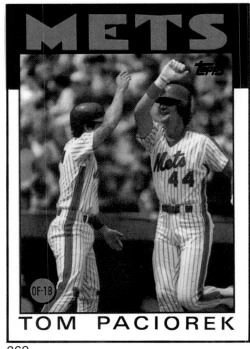

OF-1B

TOM PACIOREK

362

BRAVES

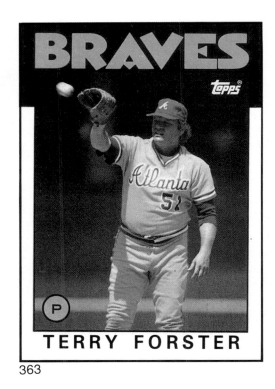

Ⓟ

TERRY FORSTER

363

WHITE SOX

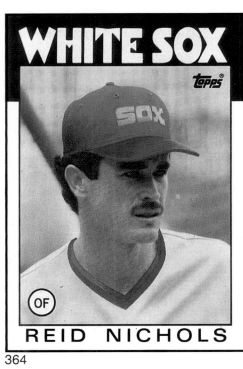

OF

REID NICHOLS

364

ORIOLES

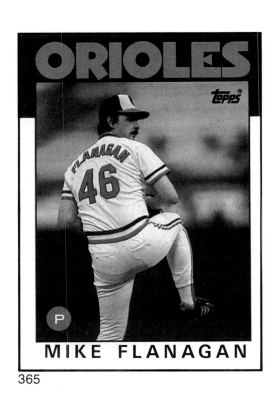

Ⓟ

MIKE FLANAGAN

365

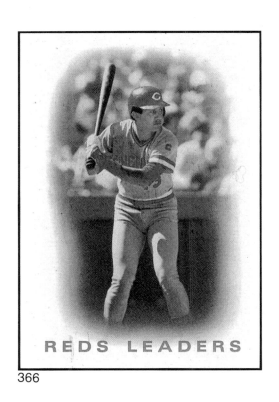

REDS LEADERS

366

TIGERS

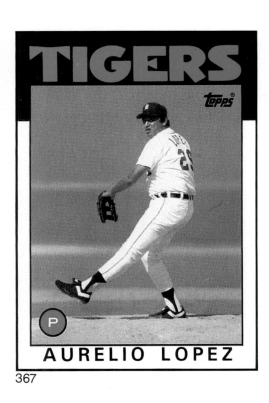

Ⓟ

AURELIO LOPEZ

367

DODGERS

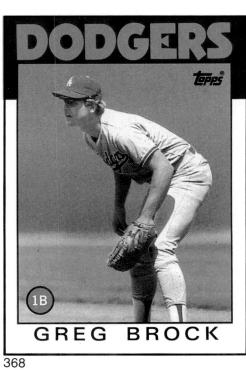

1B

GREG BROCK

368

ANGELS

Ⓟ

AL HOLLAND

369

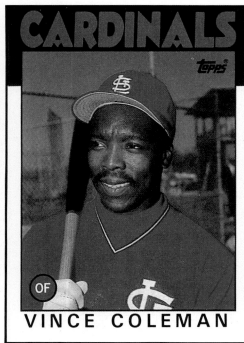

CARDINALS

VINCE COLEMAN

OF

370

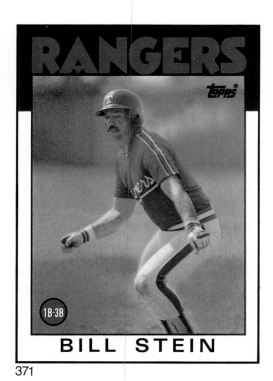

RANGERS

BILL STEIN

1B-3B

371

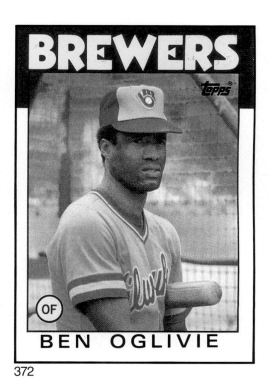

BREWERS

BEN OGLIVIE

OF

372

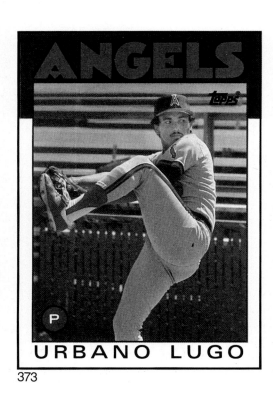

ANGELS

URBANO LUGO

P

373

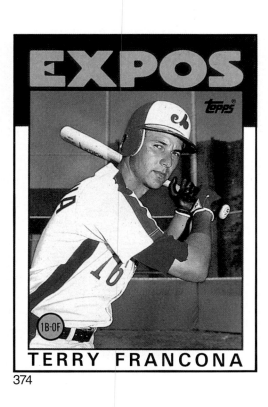

EXPOS

TERRY FRANCONA

1B-OF

374

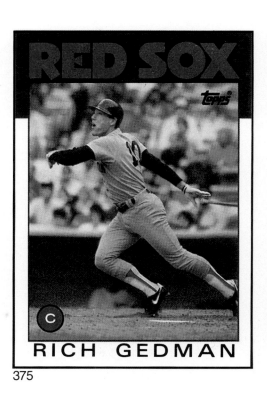

RED SOX

RICH GEDMAN

C

375

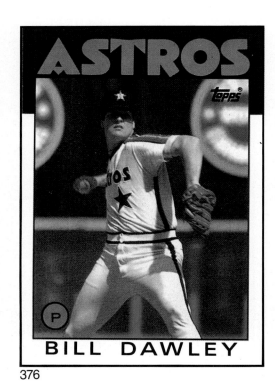

ASTROS

BILL DAWLEY

P

376

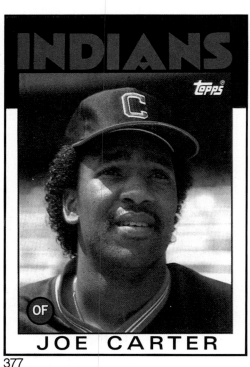

INDIANS

JOE CARTER

OF

377

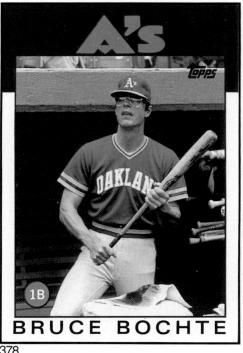

A's

BRUCE BOCHTE

1B

378

YANKEES
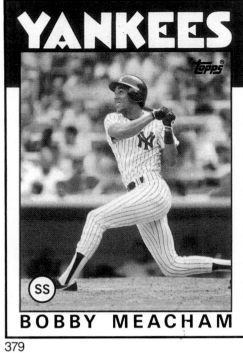
SS
BOBBY MEACHAM
379

PADRES
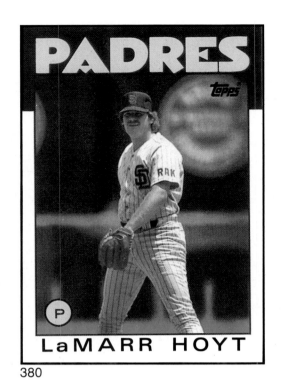
P
LaMARR HOYT
380

TWINS
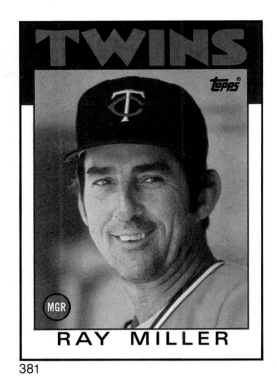
MGR
RAY MILLER
381

MARINERS
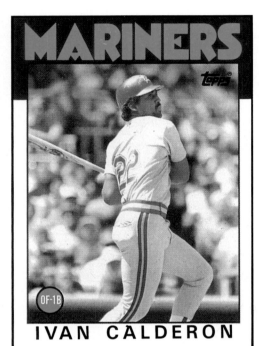
OF-1B
IVAN CALDERON
382

GIANTS
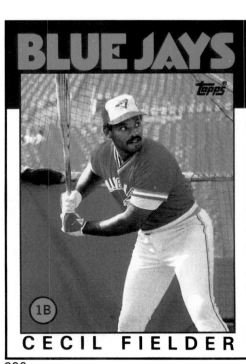
3B
CHRIS BROWN
383

CUBS

P
STEVE TROUT
384

BREWERS
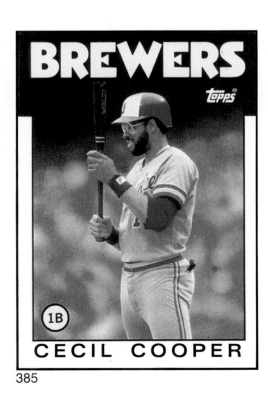
1B
CECIL COOPER
385

BLUE JAYS
1B
CECIL FIELDER
386

PIRATES
OF
STEVE KEMP
387

RANGERS

P

DICKIE NOLES

388

ASTROS

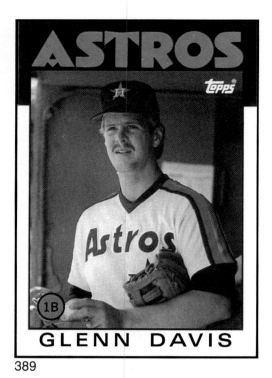

1B

GLENN DAVIS

389

WHITE SOX

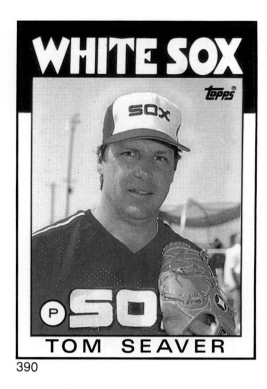

P

TOM SEAVER

390

INDIANS

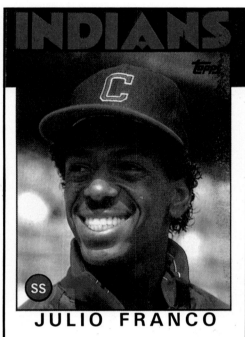

SS

JULIO FRANCO

391

PHILLIES

OF-1B

JOHN RUSSELL

392

TIGERS

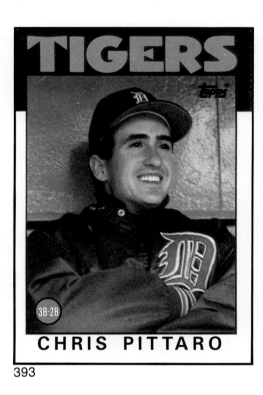

3B-2B

CHRIS PITTARO

393

1986 BASEBALL CHECKLIST Topps CARDS 265-396

265 ☐ RON DAVIS	297 ☐ TIM LOLLAR
266 ☐ KEITH MORELAND	298 ☐ CRAIG REYNOLDS
267 ☐ PAUL MOLITOR	299 ☐ BRYN SMITH
268 ☐ MIKE SCOTT	300 ☐ GEORGE BRETT
269 ☐ DANE IORG	301 ☐ DENNIS RASMUSSEN
270 ☐ JACK MORRIS	302 ☐ GREG GROSS
271 ☐ DAVE COLLINS	303 ☐ CURT WARDLE
272 ☐ TIM TOLMAN	304 ☐ MIKE GALLEGO
273 ☐ JERRY WILLARD	305 ☐ PHIL BRADLEY
274 ☐ RON GARDENHIRE	306 ☐ PADRES LEADERS
275 ☐ CHARLIE HOUGH	307 ☐ DAVE SAX
276 ☐ YANKEES LEADERS	308 ☐ RAY FONTENOT
277 ☐ JAIME COCANOWER	309 ☐ JOHN SHELBY
278 ☐ SIXTO LEZCANO	310 ☐ GREG MINTON
279 ☐ AL PARDO	311 ☐ DICK SCHOFIELD
280 ☐ TIM RAINES	312 ☐ TOM FILER
281 ☐ STEVE MURA	313 ☐ JOE DE SA
282 ☐ JERRY MUMPHREY	314 ☐ FRANK PASTORE
283 ☐ MIKE FISCHLIN	315 ☐ MOOKIE WILSON
284 ☐ BRIAN DAYETT	316 ☐ SAMMY KHALIFA
285 ☐ BUDDY BELL	317 ☐ ED ROMERO
286 ☐ LUIS DeLEON	318 ☐ TERRY WHITFIELD
287 ☐ JOHN CHRISTENSEN	319 ☐ RICK CAMP
288 ☐ DON AASE	320 ☐ JIM RICE
289 ☐ JOHNNIE LeMASTER	321 ☐ EARL WEAVER
290 ☐ CARLTON FISK	322 ☐ BOB FORSCH
291 ☐ TOM LASORDA	323 ☐ JERRY DAVIS
292 ☐ CHUCK PORTER	324 ☐ DAN SCHATZEDER
293 ☐ CHRIS CHAMBLISS	325 ☐ JUAN BENIQUEZ
294 ☐ DANNY COX	326 ☐ KENT TEKULVE
295 ☐ KIRK GIBSON	327 ☐ MIKE PAGLIARULO
296 ☐ GENO PETRALLI	328 ☐ PETE O'BRIEN

394

GIANTS

P

SCOTT GARRELTS

395

RED SOX LEADERS

396

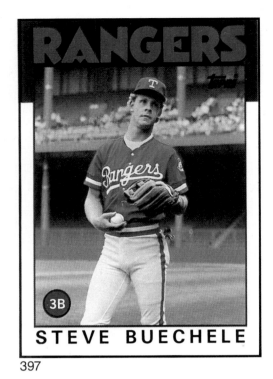

STEVE BUECHELE
397

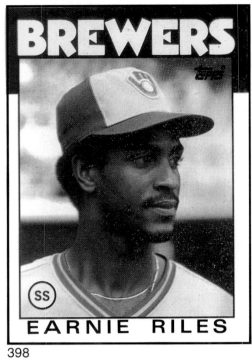

EARNIE RILES
398

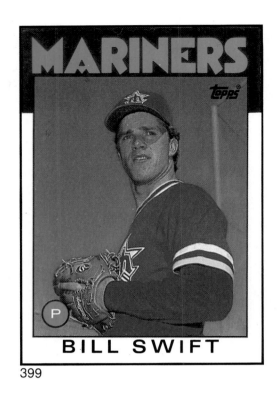

BILL SWIFT
399

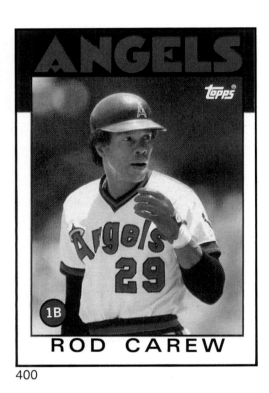

ROD CAREW
400

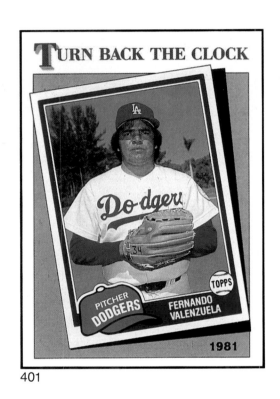

TURN BACK THE CLOCK

FERNANDO VALENZUELA

1981

401

TURN BACK THE CLOCK

TOM SEAVER
METS

1976

402

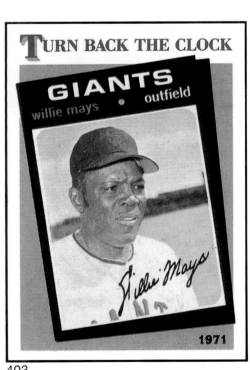

TURN BACK THE CLOCK

GIANTS • outfield
willie mays

1971

403

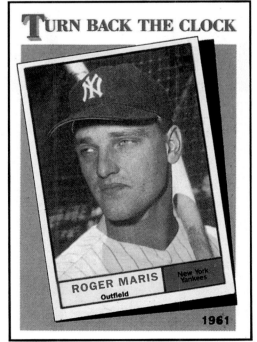

TURN BACK THE CLOCK

ORIOLES

FRANK ROBINSON outfield

1966

404

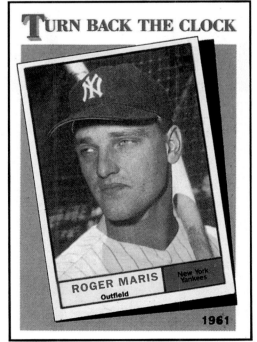

TURN BACK THE CLOCK

ROGER MARIS
Outfield

1961

405

CUBS

SCOTT SANDERSON

406

EXPOS
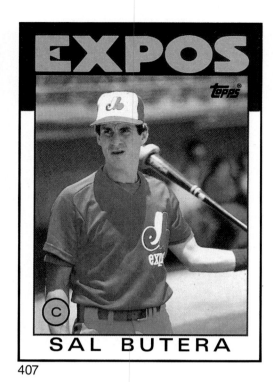

SAL BUTERA

407

ASTROS
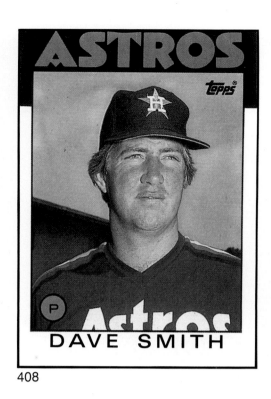

DAVE SMITH

408

BRAVES
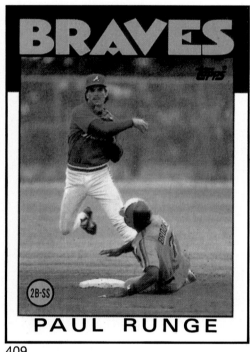

PAUL RUNGE

409

A's
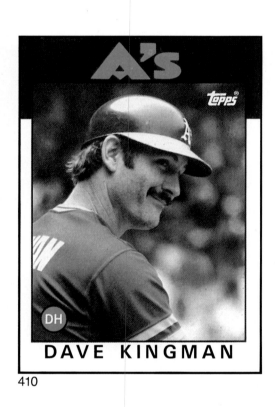

DAVE KINGMAN

410

TIGERS
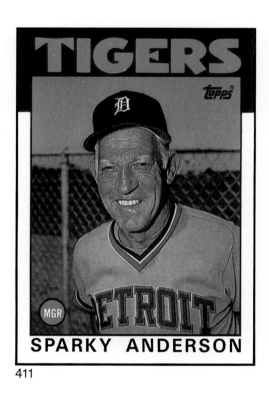

SPARKY ANDERSON

411

BLUE JAYS
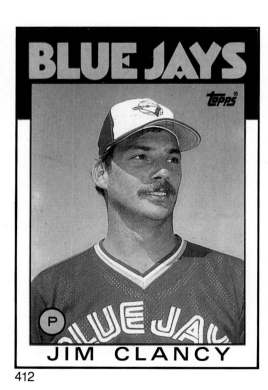

JIM CLANCY

412

PADRES

TIM FLANNERY

413

METS
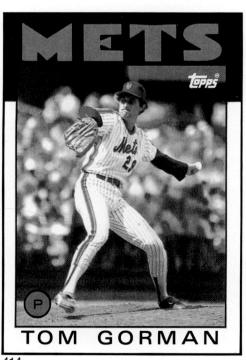

TOM GORMAN

414

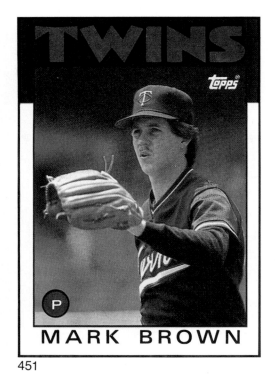

TWINS

MARK BROWN

P

451

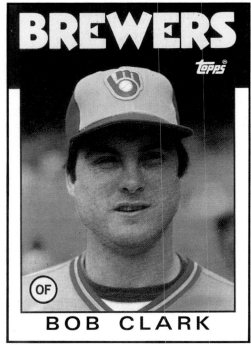

BREWERS

BOB CLARK

OF

452

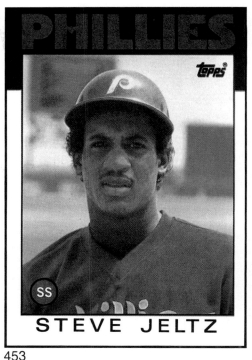

PHILLIES

STEVE JELTZ

SS

453

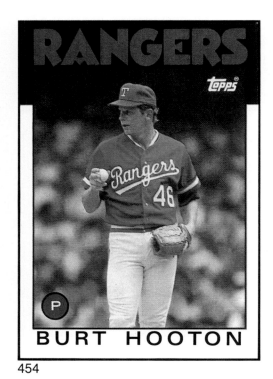

RANGERS

BURT HOOTON

P

454

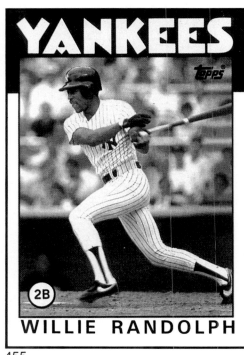

YANKEES

WILLIE RANDOLPH

2B

455

BRAVES LEADERS

456

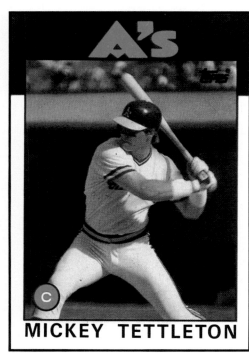

A's

MICKEY TETTLETON

C

457

ASTROS

KEVIN BASS

OF

458

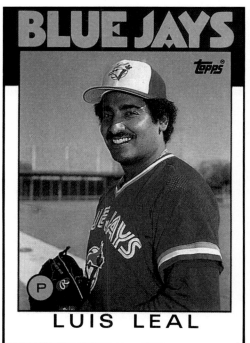

BLUE JAYS

LUIS LEAL

P

459

CUBS
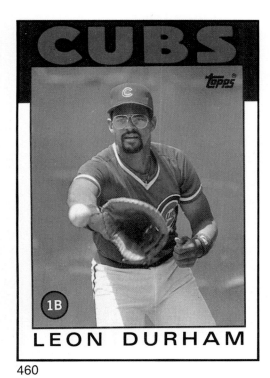
LEON DURHAM
460

TIGERS
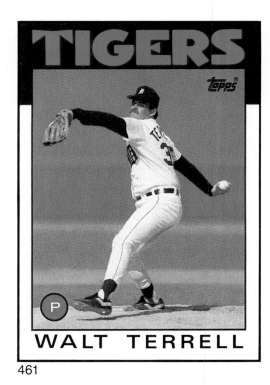
WALT TERRELL
461

MARINERS
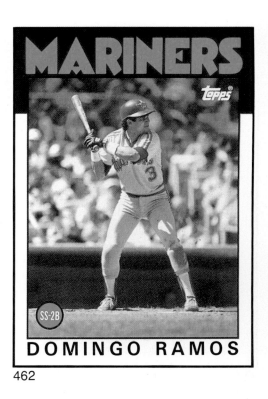
DOMINGO RAMOS
462

GIANTS
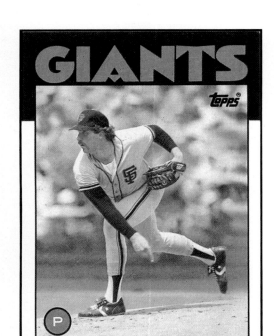
JIM GOTT
463

ANGELS
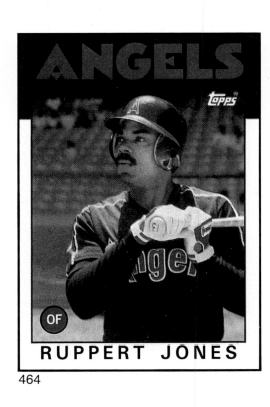
RUPPERT JONES
464

METS
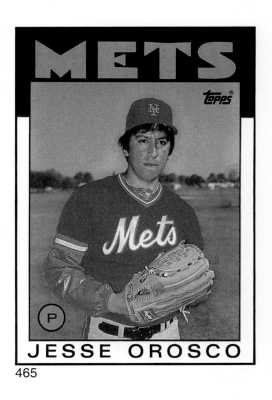
JESSE OROSCO
465

PHILLIES
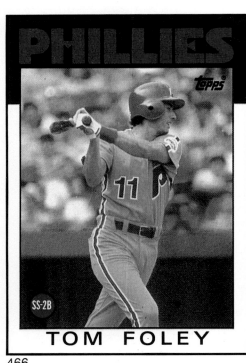
TOM FOLEY
466

WHITE SOX
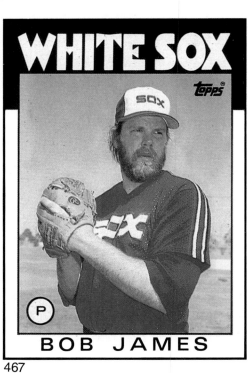
BOB JAMES
467

DODGERS
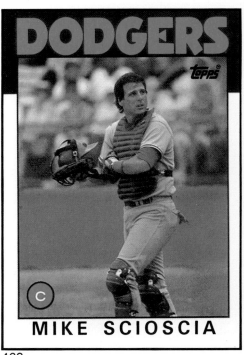
MIKE SCIOSCIA
468

ORIOLES

STORM DAVIS

469

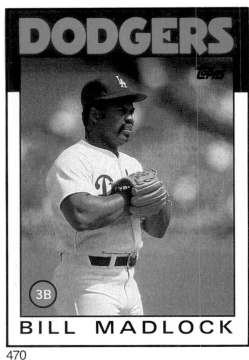

DODGERS

BILL MADLOCK

470

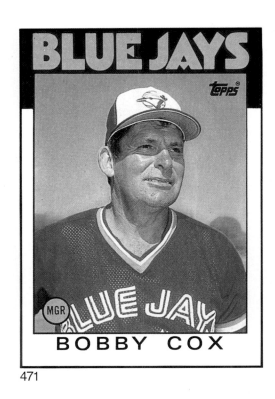

BLUE JAYS

BOBBY COX

471

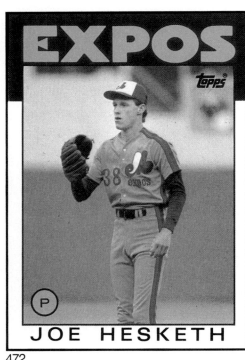

EXPOS

JOE HESKETH

472

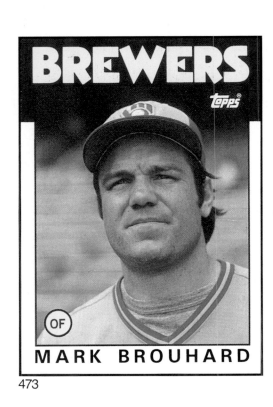

BREWERS

MARK BROUHARD

473

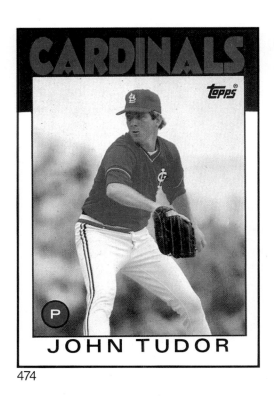

CARDINALS

JOHN TUDOR

474

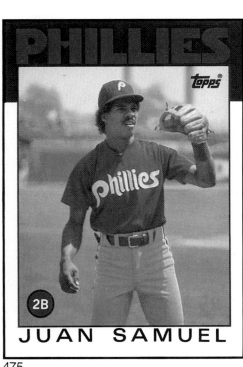

PHILLIES

JUAN SAMUEL

475

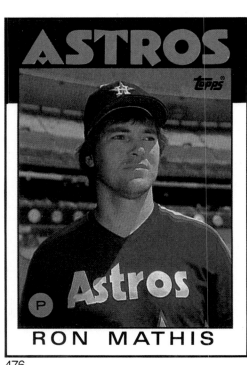

ASTROS

RON MATHIS

476

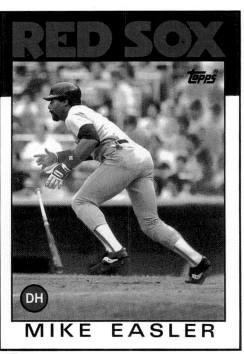

RED SOX

MIKE EASLER

477

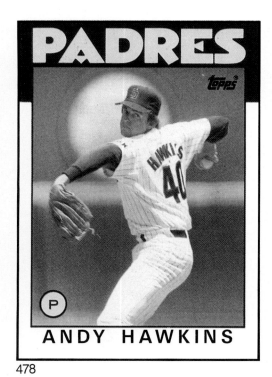

PADRES

ANDY HAWKINS

478

TIGERS

BOB MELVIN

479

RANGERS

ODDIBE McDOWELL

480

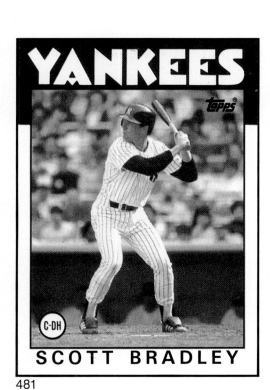

YANKEES

SCOTT BRADLEY

481

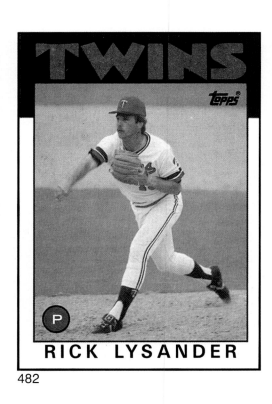

TWINS

RICK LYSANDER

482

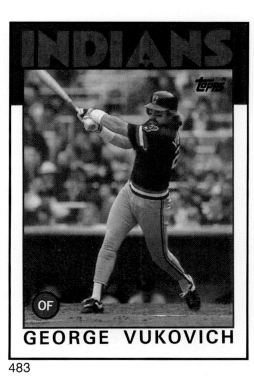

INDIANS

GEORGE VUKOVICH

483

A's

DONNIE HILL

484

CUBS

GARY MATTHEWS

485

ANGELS LEADERS

486

ROYALS

BRET SABERHAGEN
487

BLUE JAYS

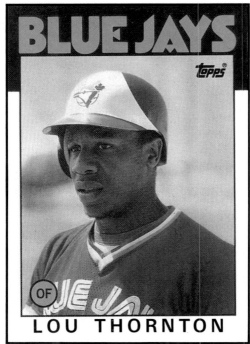

LOU THORNTON
488

PIRATES

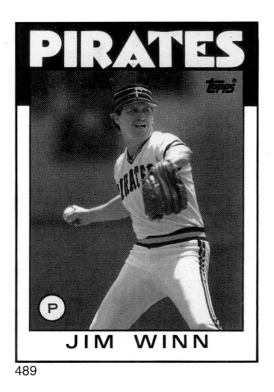

JIM WINN
489

GIANTS

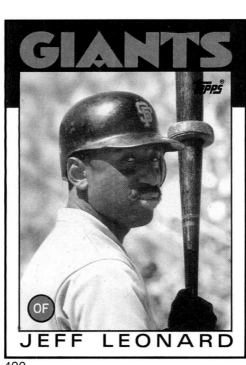

JEFF LEONARD
490

BRAVES

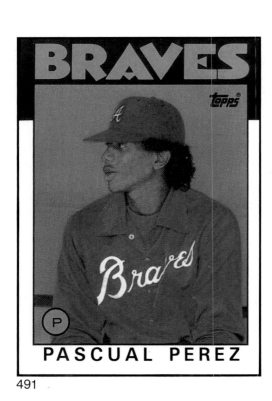

PASCUAL PEREZ
491

METS

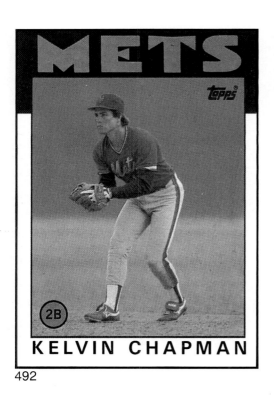

KELVIN CHAPMAN
492

WHITE SOX

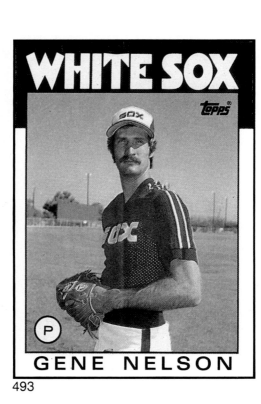

GENE NELSON
493

ORIOLES

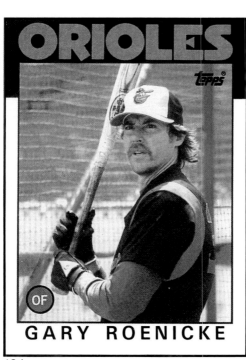

GARY ROENICKE
494

MARINERS

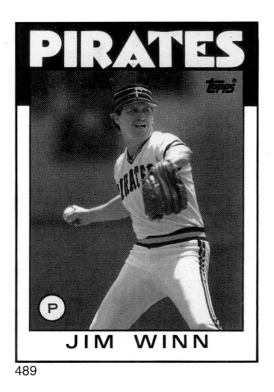

MARK LANGSTON
495

DODGERS

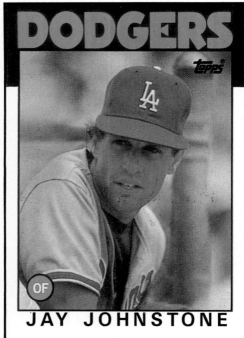

OF

JAY JOHNSTONE

496

REDS

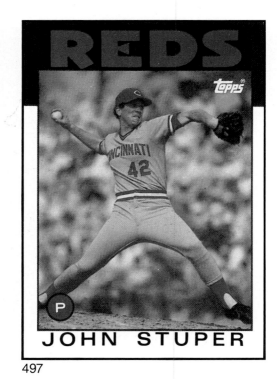

P

JOHN STUPER

497

CARDINALS

OF

TITO LANDRUM

498

BREWERS

P

BOB GIBSON

499

YANKEES

OF

RICKEY HENDERSON

500

METS

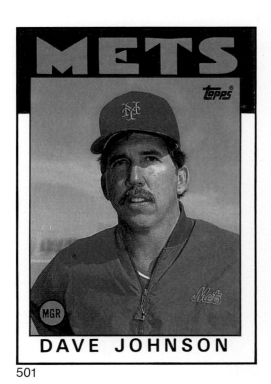

MGR

DAVE JOHNSON

501

RANGERS

P

GLEN COOK

502

EXPOS

MIKE FITZGERALD

C

503

ASTROS

1B-OF

DENNY WALLING

504

PHILLIES

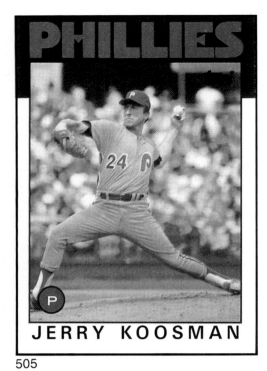

JERRY KOOSMAN

505

DODGERS

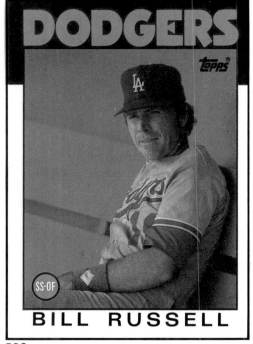

BILL RUSSELL

506

A'S

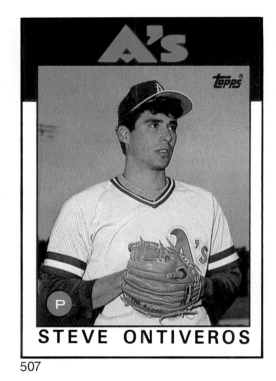

STEVE ONTIVEROS

507

ORIOLES

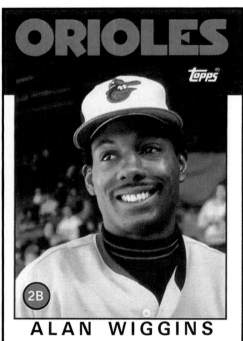

ALAN WIGGINS

508

INDIANS

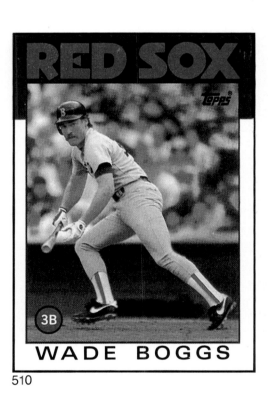

ERNIE CAMACHO

509

RED SOX

WADE BOGGS

510

MARINERS

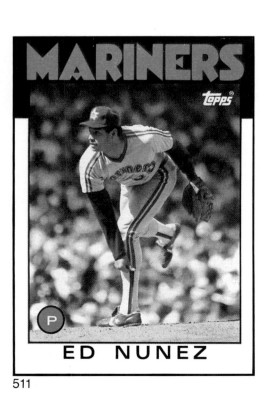

ED NUNEZ

511

CUBS

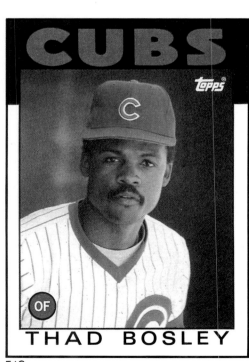

THAD BOSLEY

512

TWINS

RON WASHINGTON

513

ROYALS
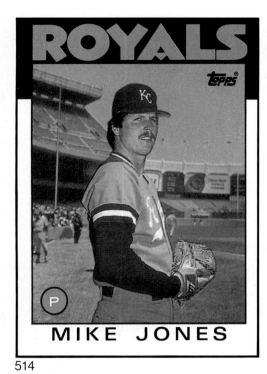
MIKE JONES
514

TIGERS
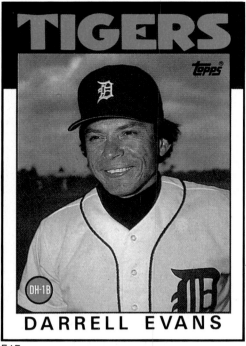
DARRELL EVANS
515

GIANTS LEADERS
516

BRAVES
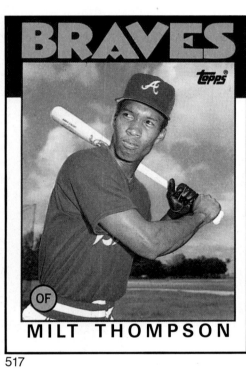
MILT THOMPSON
517

BLUE JAYS
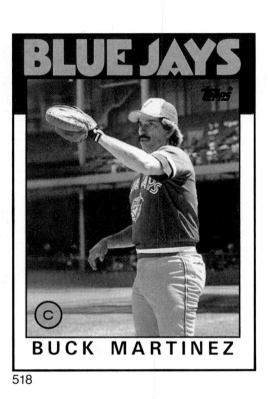
BUCK MARTINEZ
518

BREWERS
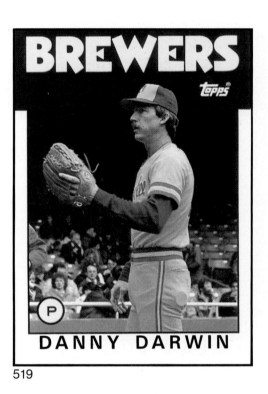
DANNY DARWIN
519

METS
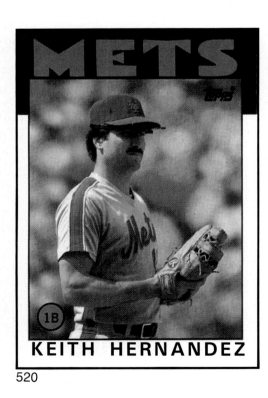
KEITH HERNANDEZ
520

ORIOLES
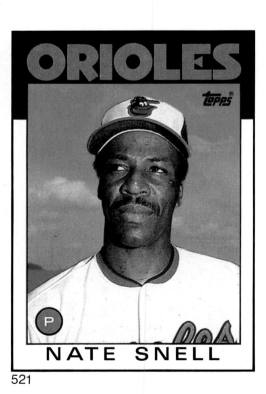
NATE SNELL
521

DODGERS
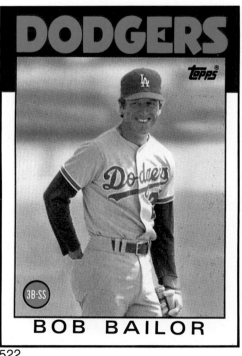
BOB BAILOR
522

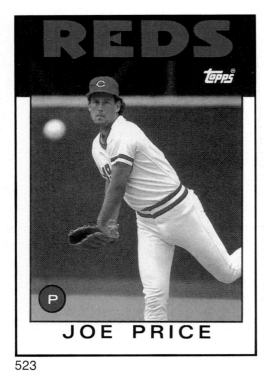

REDS

JOE PRICE

523

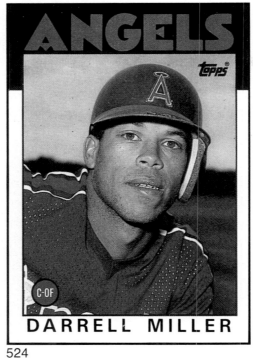

ANGELS

DARRELL MILLER

524

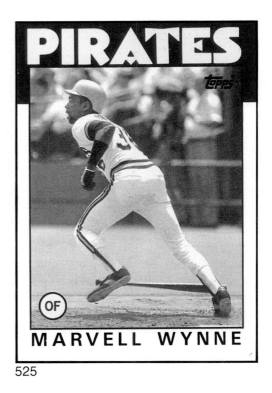

PIRATES

MARVELL WYNNE

525

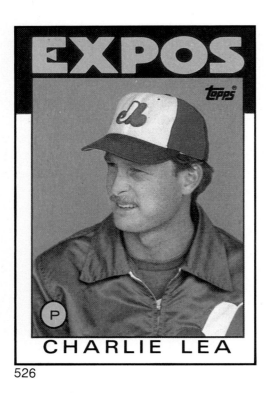

EXPOS

CHARLIE LEA

526

1986 BASEBALL CHECKLIST

Topps CARDS 397-528

397 ☐ STEVE BUECHELE	429 ☐ GREG BOOKER
398 ☐ EARNIE RILES	430 ☐ KENT HRBEK
399 ☐ BILL SWIFT	431 ☐ GEORGE FRAZIER
400 ☐ ROD CAREW	432 ☐ MARK BAILEY
401 ☐ TURN BACK — 1981	433 ☐ CHRIS CODIROLI
402 ☐ TURN BACK — 1976	434 ☐ CURT WILKERSON
403 ☐ TURN BACK — 1971	435 ☐ BILL CAUDILL
404 ☐ TURN BACK — 1966	436 ☐ DOUG FLYNN
405 ☐ TURN BACK — 1961	437 ☐ RICK MAHLER
406 ☐ SCOTT SANDERSON	438 ☐ CLINT HURDLE
407 ☐ SAL BUTERA	439 ☐ RICK HONEYCUTT
408 ☐ DAVE SMITH	440 ☐ ALVIN DAVIS
409 ☐ PAUL RUNGE	441 ☐ WHITEY HERZOG
410 ☐ DAVE KINGMAN	442 ☐ RON ROBINSON
411 ☐ SPARKY ANDERSON	443 ☐ BILL BUCKNER
412 ☐ JIM CLANCY	444 ☐ ALEX TREVINO
413 ☐ TIM FLANNERY	445 ☐ BERT BLYLEVEN
414 ☐ TOM GORMAN	446 ☐ LENN SAKATA
415 ☐ HAL McRAE	447 ☐ JERRY DON GLEATON
416 ☐ DENNY MARTINEZ	448 ☐ HERM WINNINGHAM
417 ☐ R.J. REYNOLDS	449 ☐ ROD SCURRY
418 ☐ ALAN KNICELY	450 ☐ GRAIG NETTLES
419 ☐ FRANK WILLS	451 ☐ MARK BROWN
420 ☐ VON HAYES	452 ☐ BOB CLARK
421 ☐ DAVE PALMER	453 ☐ STEVE JELTZ
422 ☐ MIKE JORGENSEN	454 ☐ BURT HOOTON
423 ☐ DAN SPILLNER	455 ☐ WILLIE RANDOLPH
424 ☐ RICK MILLER	456 ☐ BRAVES LEADERS
425 ☐ LARRY McWILLIAMS	457 ☐ MICKEY TETTLETON
426 ☐ BREWERS LEADERS	458 ☐ KEVIN BASS
427 ☐ JOE COWLEY	459 ☐ LUIS LEAL
428 ☐ MAX VENABLE	460 ☐ LEON DURHAM

527

CARDINALS

TERRY PENDLETON

528

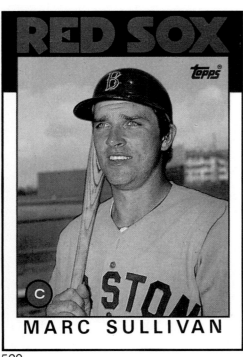

RED SOX

MARC SULLIVAN

529

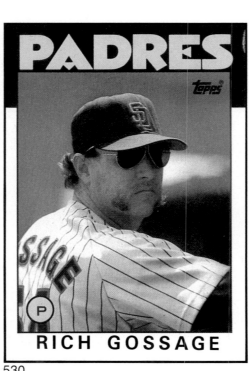

PADRES

RICH GOSSAGE

530

WHITE SOX

TONY LaRUSSA

531

PHILLIES
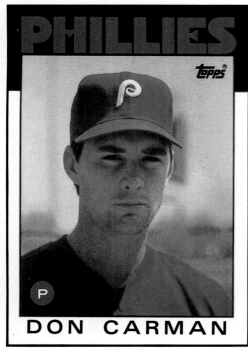
DON CARMAN
P
532

YANKEES
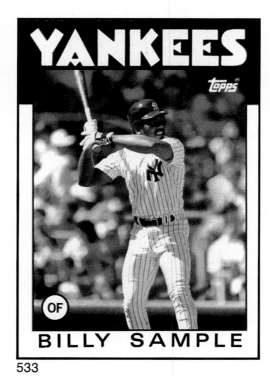
BILLY SAMPLE
OF
533

ASTROS
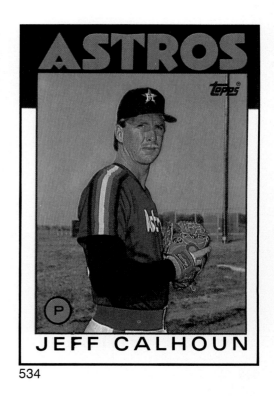
JEFF CALHOUN
P
534

RANGERS
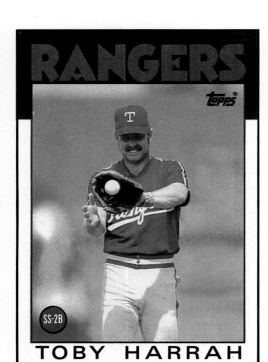
TOBY HARRAH
SS-2B
535

A's
JOSE RIJO
P
536

TWINS
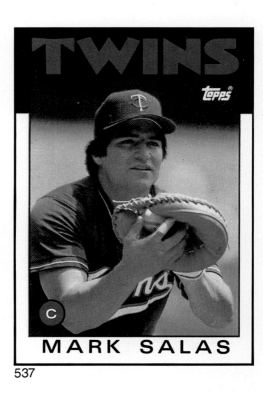
MARK SALAS
C
537

CUBS
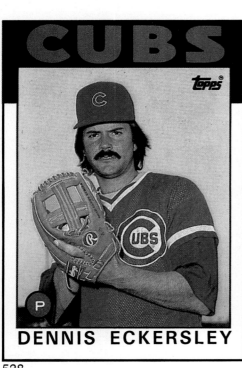
DENNIS ECKERSLEY
P
538

BRAVES
GLENN HUBBARD
2B
539

TIGERS
DAN PETRY
P
540

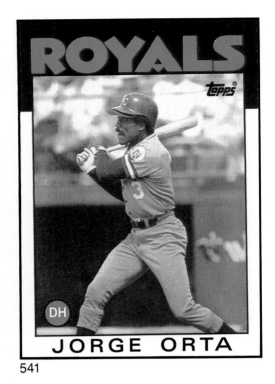

JORGE ORTA

541

DON SCHULZE

542

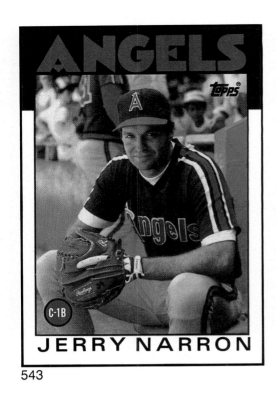

JERRY NARRON

543

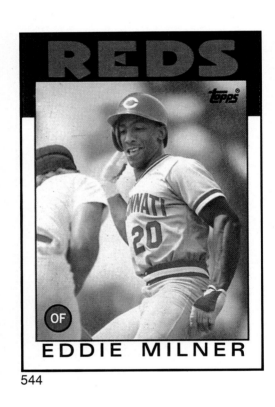

EDDIE MILNER

544

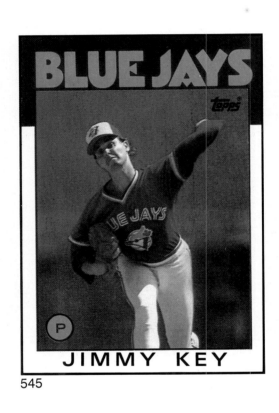

JIMMY KEY

545

MARINERS LEADERS

546

ROGER McDOWELL

547

MIKE YOUNG

548

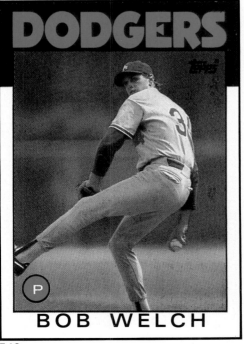

BOB WELCH

549

CARDINALS

2B

TOM HERR

550

GIANTS

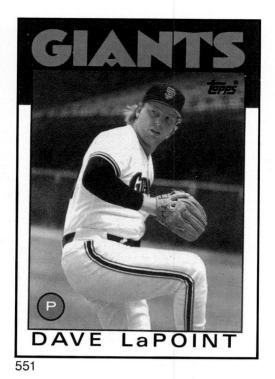

P

DAVE LaPOINT

551

WHITE SOX

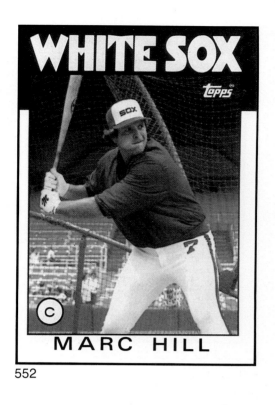

C

MARC HILL

552

PIRATES

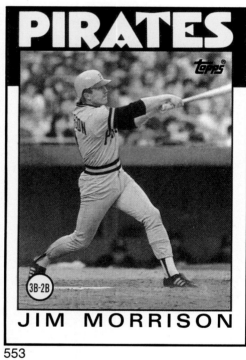

3B-2B

JIM MORRISON

553

BREWERS

PAUL HOUSEHOLDER

OF

554

EXPOS

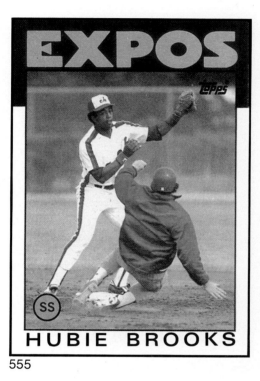

SS

HUBIE BROOKS

555

PHILLIES

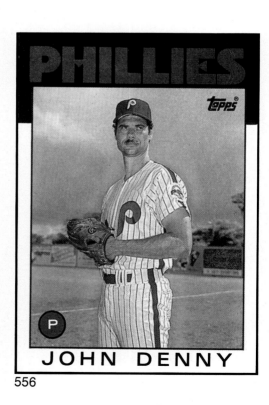

P

JOHN DENNY

556

BRAVES

1B

GERALD PERRY

557

PADRES

P

TIM STODDARD

558

RANGERS
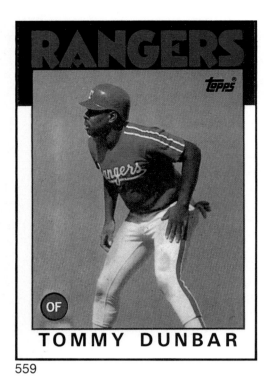
TOMMY DUNBAR
OF
559

YANKEES
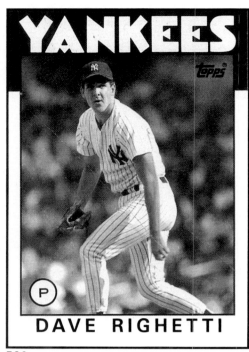
DAVE RIGHETTI
P
560

ASTROS
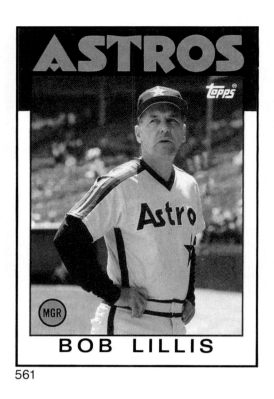
BOB LILLIS
MGR
561

ROYALS
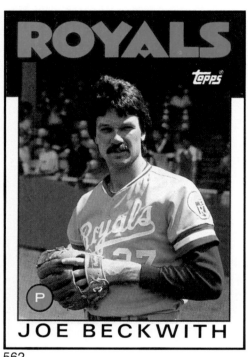
JOE BECKWITH
P
562

TIGERS

ALEJANDRO SANCHEZ
DH-OF
563

CUBS
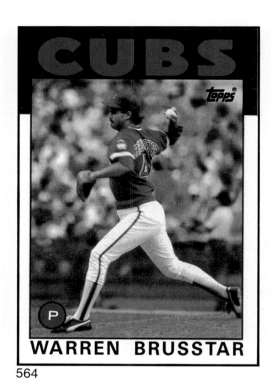
WARREN BRUSSTAR
P
564

TWINS

TOM BRUNANSKY
OF
565

A's
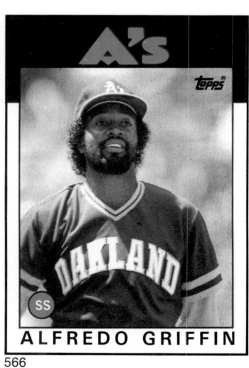
ALFREDO GRIFFIN
SS
566

INDIANS
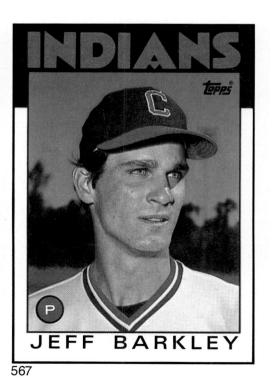
JEFF BARKLEY
P
567

MARINERS
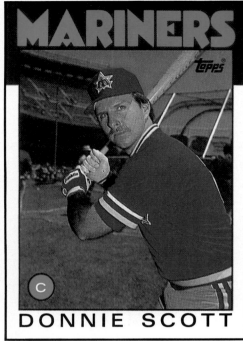
DONNIE SCOTT
568

BLUE JAYS
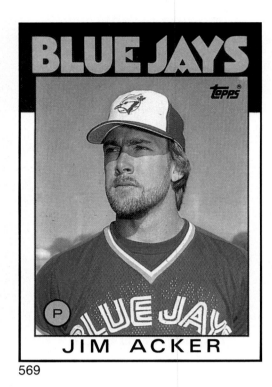
JIM ACKER
569

METS
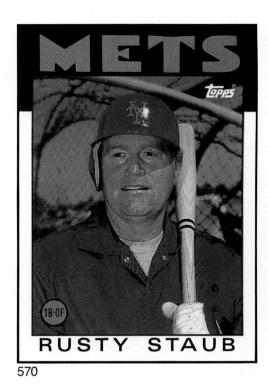
RUSTY STAUB
570

GIANTS
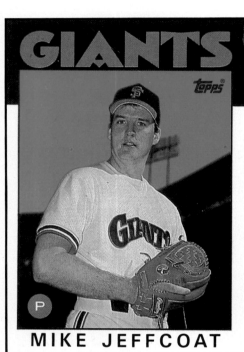
MIKE JEFFCOAT
571

BRAVES
PAUL ZUVELLA
572

REDS
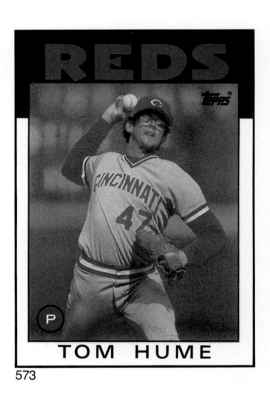
TOM HUME
573

WHITE SOX
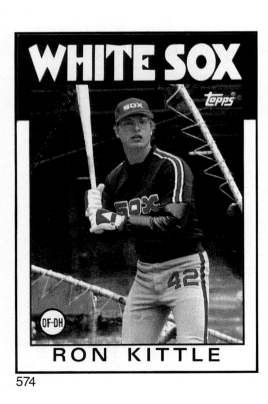
RON KITTLE
574

ORIOLES
MIKE BODDICKER
575

EXPOS LEADERS
576

DODGERS

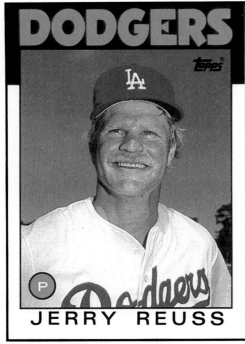

JERRY REUSS

577

PIRATES

LEE MAZZILLI

578

ANGELS

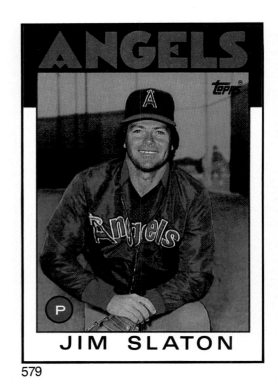

JIM SLATON

579

CARDINALS

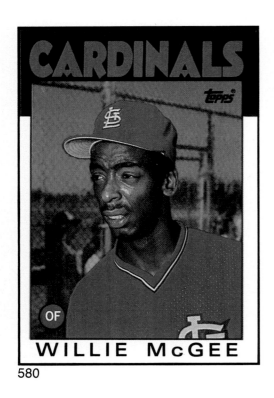

WILLIE McGEE

580

RED SOX

Topps

BRUCE HURST

581

BREWERS

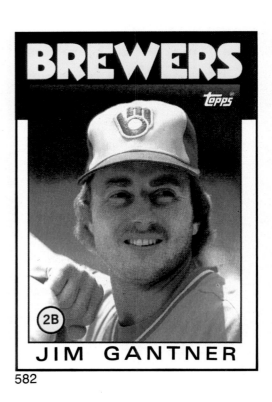

JIM GANTNER

582

PADRES

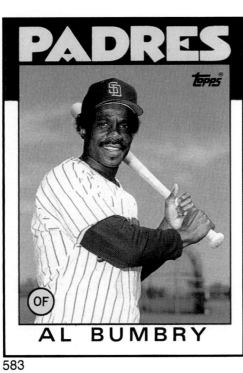

AL BUMBRY

583

YANKEES

BRIAN FISHER

584

PHILLIES

GARRY MADDOX

585

RANGERS
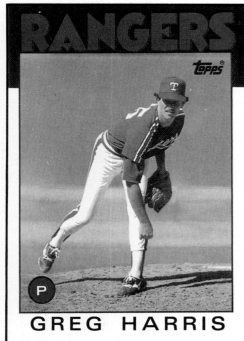
GREG HARRIS
586

METS
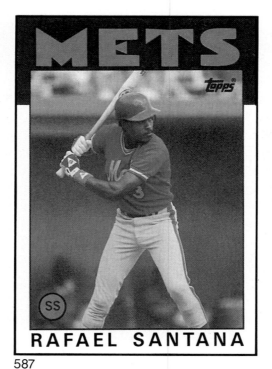
RAFAEL SANTANA
587

CUBS
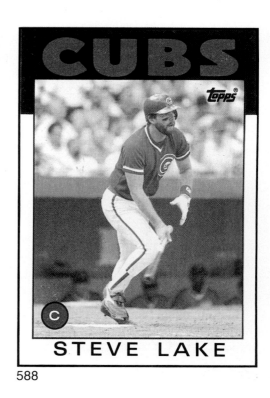
STEVE LAKE
588

PIRATES
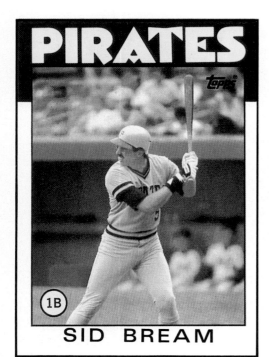
SID BREAM
589

ASTROS

BOB KNEPPER
590

A's
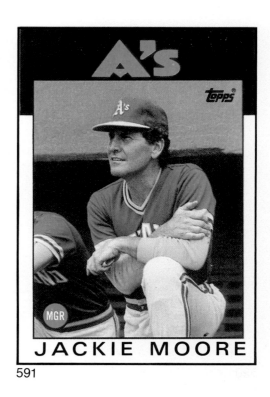
JACKIE MOORE
591

TIGERS
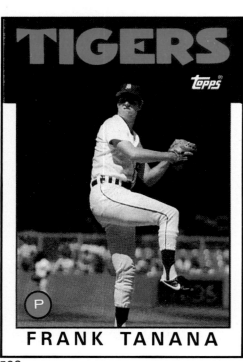
FRANK TANANA
592

BLUE JAYS
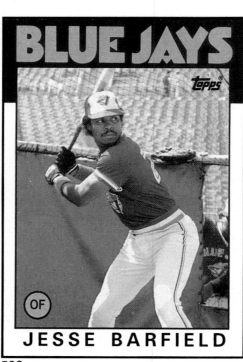
JESSE BARFIELD
593

INDIANS
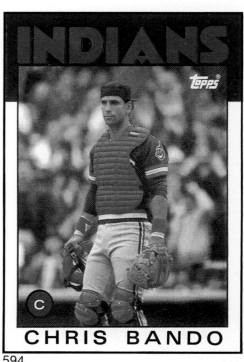
CHRIS BANDO
594

REDS

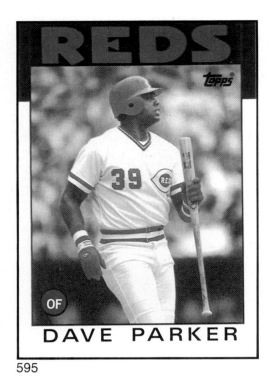

OF

DAVE PARKER

595

ROYALS

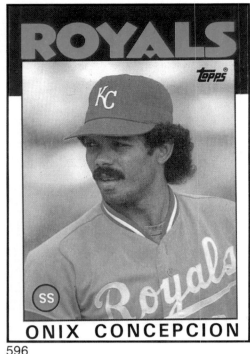

SS

ONIX CONCEPCION

596

ORIOLES

P

SAMMY STEWART

597

MARINERS

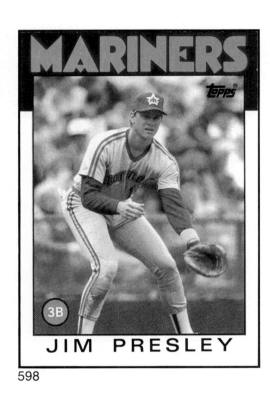

3B

JIM PRESLEY

598

METS

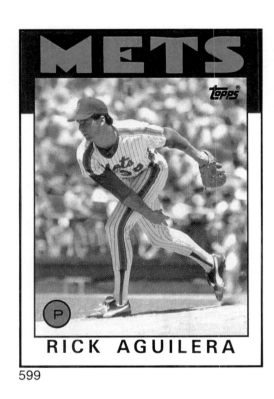

P

RICK AGUILERA

599

BRAVES

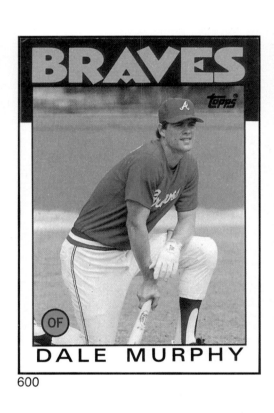

OF

DALE MURPHY

600

EXPOS

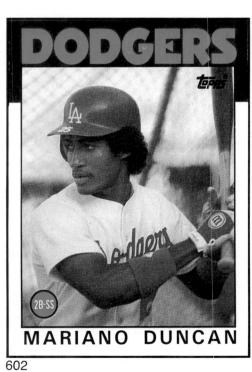

P

GARY LUCAS

601

DODGERS

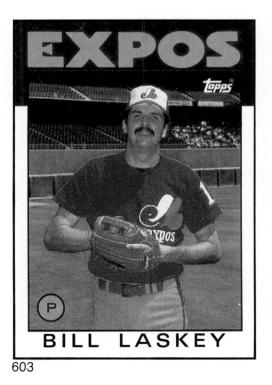

2B-SS

MARIANO DUNCAN

602

EXPOS

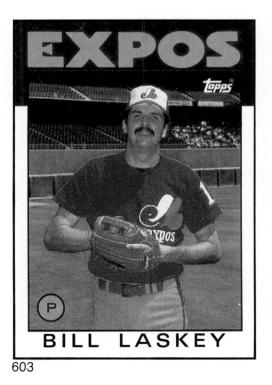

P

BILL LASKEY

603

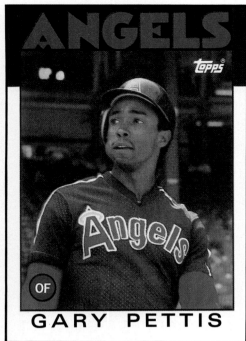

ANGELS

GARY PETTIS

OF

604

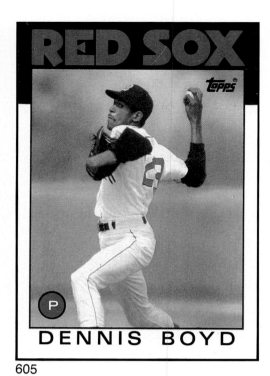

RED SOX

DENNIS BOYD

P

605

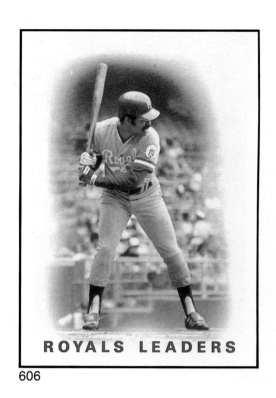

ROYALS LEADERS

606

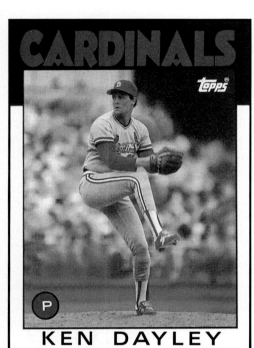

CARDINALS

KEN DAYLEY

P

607

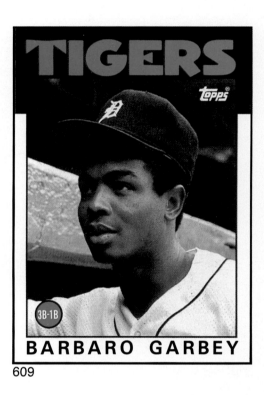

PADRES

BRUCE BOCHY

C

608

Tigers

BARBARO GARBEY

3B-1B

609

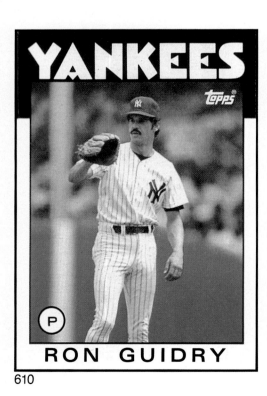

YANKEES

RON GUIDRY

P

610

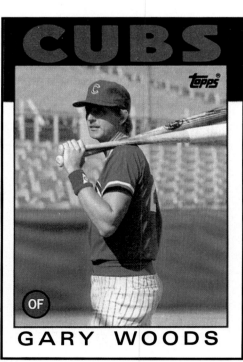

CUBS

GARY WOODS

OF

611

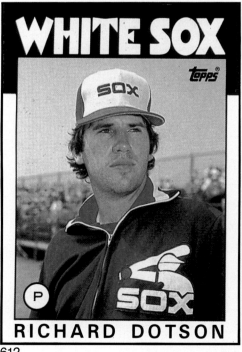

WHITE SOX

RICHARD DOTSON

P

612

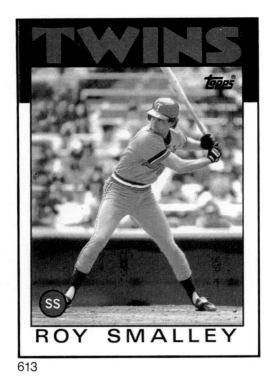

TWINS

ROY SMALLEY

613

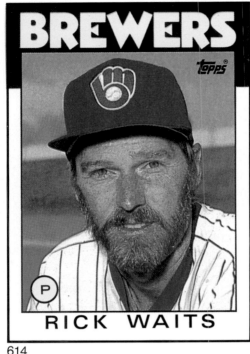

BREWERS

RICK WAITS

614

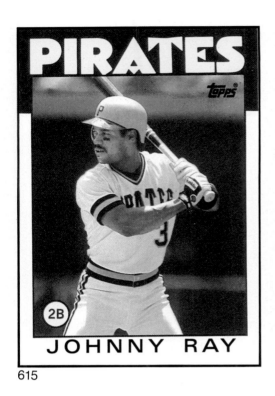

PIRATES

JOHNNY RAY

615

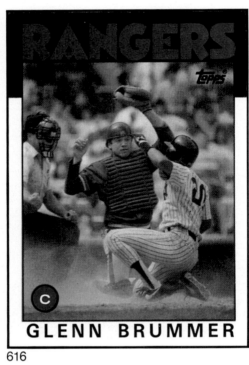

RANGERS

GLENN BRUMMER

616

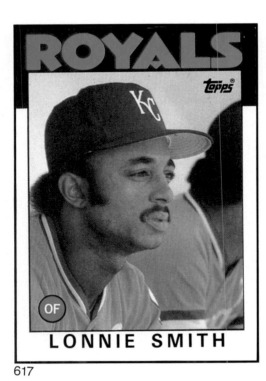

ROYALS

LONNIE SMITH

617

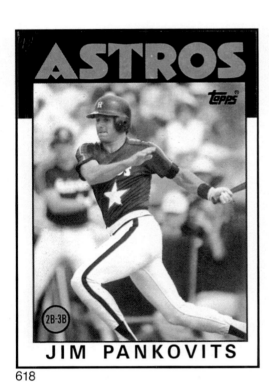

ASTROS

JIM PANKOVITS

618

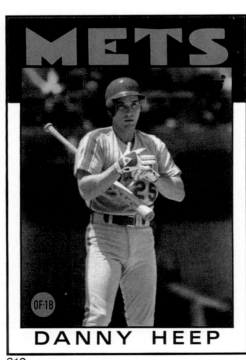

METS

DANNY HEEP

619

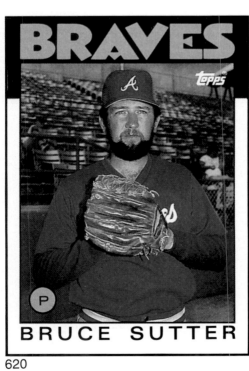

BRAVES

BRUCE SUTTER

620

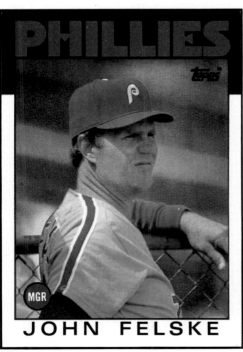

PHILLIES

JOHN FELSKE

621

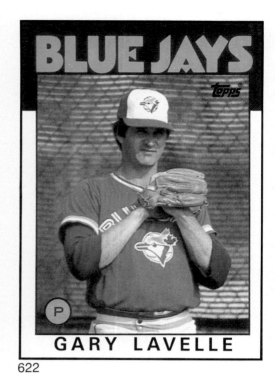

BLUE JAYS

GARY LAVELLE

622

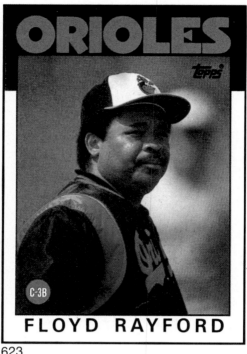

ORIOLES

FLOYD RAYFORD

623

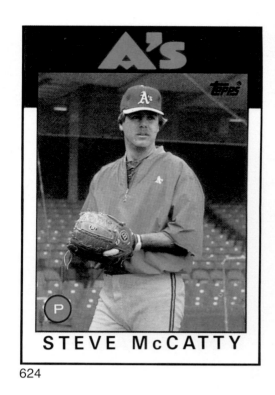

A's

STEVE McCATTY

624

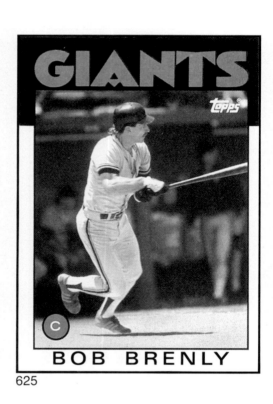

GIANTS

BOB BRENLY

625

MARINERS

ROY THOMAS

626

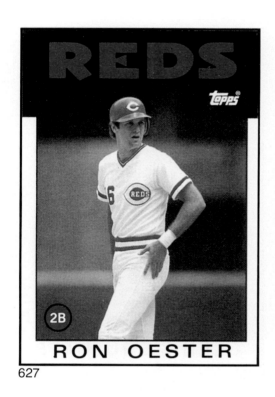

REDS

RON OESTER

627

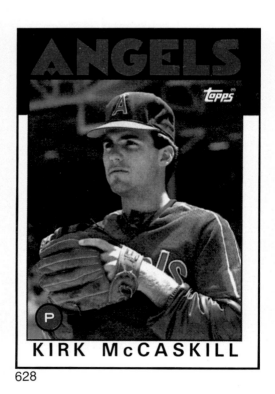

ANGELS

KIRK McCASKILL

628

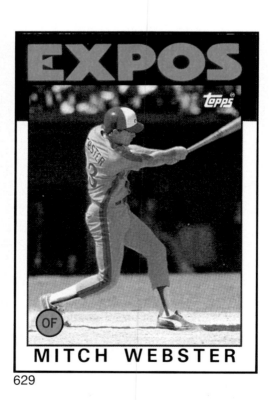

EXPOS

MITCH WEBSTER

629

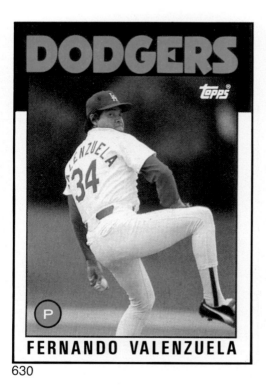

DODGERS

FERNANDO VALENZUELA

630

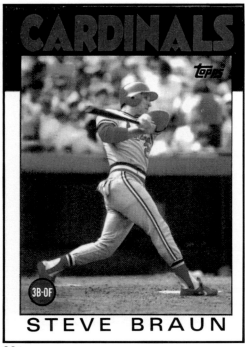

CARDINALS

STEVE BRAUN
3B-OF

631

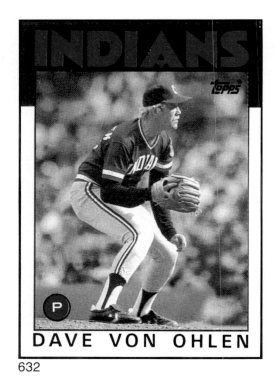

INDIANS

DAVE VON OHLEN
P

632

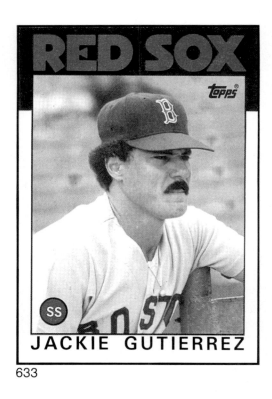

RED SOX

JACKIE GUTIERREZ
SS

633

PADRES

ROY LEE JACKSON
P

634

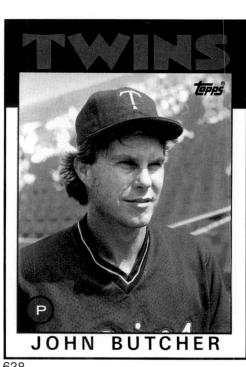

PIRATES

JASON THOMPSON
1B

635

CUBS LEADERS

636

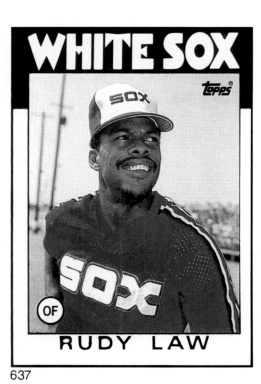

WHITE SOX

RUDY LAW
OF

637

TWINS

JOHN BUTCHER
P

638

REDS

BO DIAZ
C

639

ASTROS
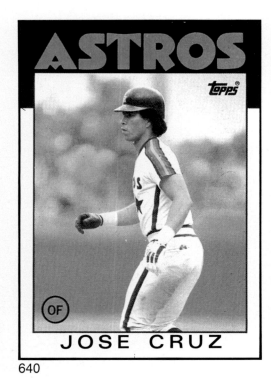
OF
JOSE CRUZ
640

RANGERS
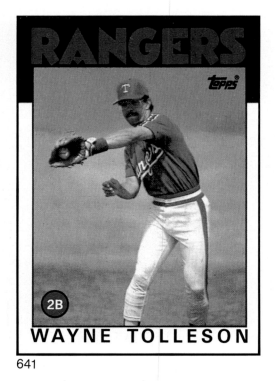
2B
WAYNE TOLLESON
641

BREWERS
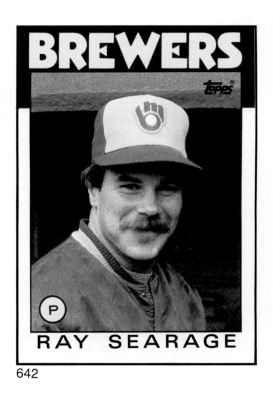
P
RAY SEARAGE
642

TIGERS

3B
TOM BROOKENS
643

ROYALS
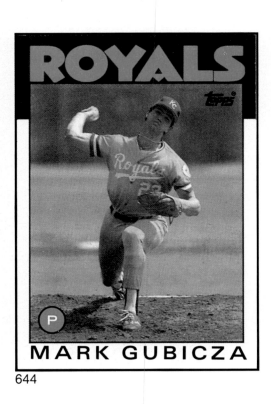
P
MARK GUBICZA
644

A's

OF-1B
DUSTY BAKER
645

MARINERS
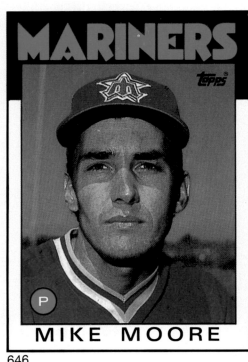
P
MIKE MOORE
646

INDIANS
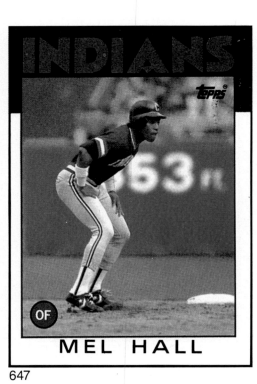
OF
MEL HALL
647

BRAVES

P
STEVE BEDROSIAN
648

METS
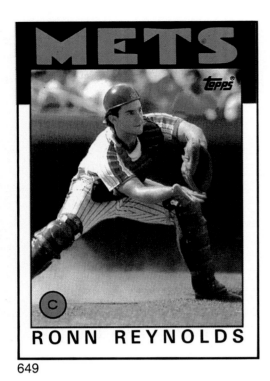
RONN REYNOLDS
649

BLUE JAYS
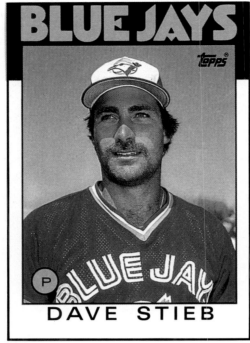
DAVE STIEB
650

YANKEES
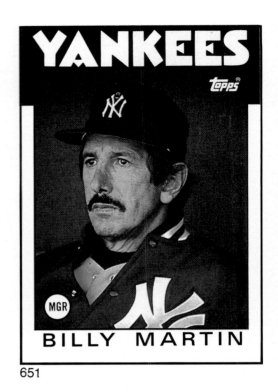
BILLY MARTIN
651

REDS
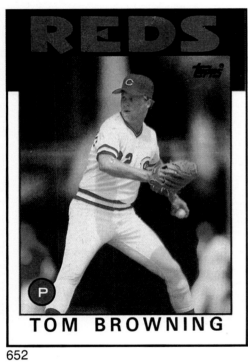
TOM BROWNING
652

ORIOLES
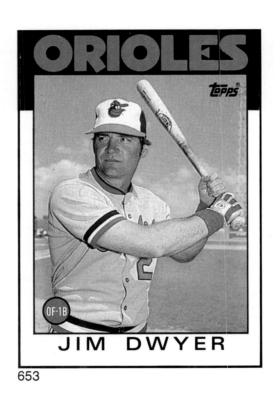
JIM DWYER
653

DODGERS
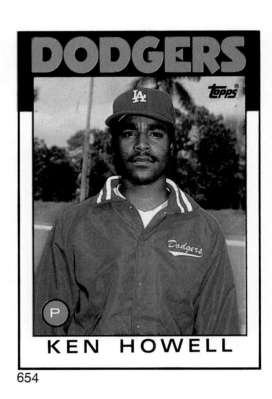
KEN HOWELL
654

GIANTS

MANNY TRILLO
655

CARDINALS
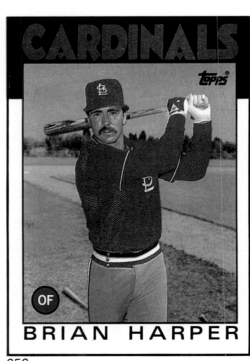
BRIAN HARPER
656

WHITE SOX

JUAN AGOSTO
657

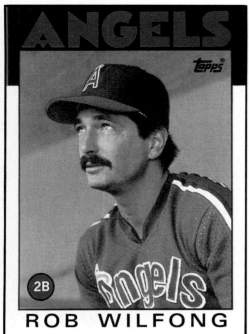

ANGELS

ROB WILFONG

658

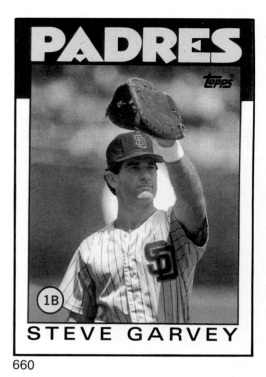

PADRES

STEVE GARVEY

660

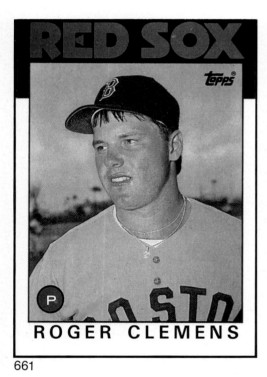

RED SOX

ROGER CLEMENS

661

BREWERS

BILL SCHROEDER

662

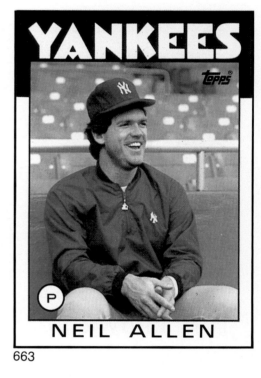

YANKEES

NEIL ALLEN

663

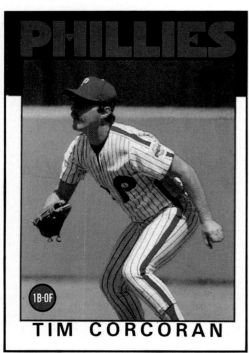

PHILLIES

TIM CORCORAN

664

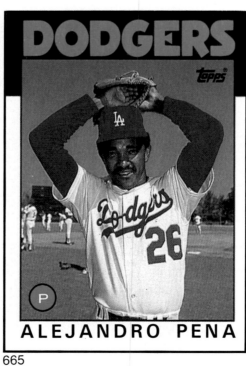

DODGERS

ALEJANDRO PENA

665

RANGERS LEADERS

666

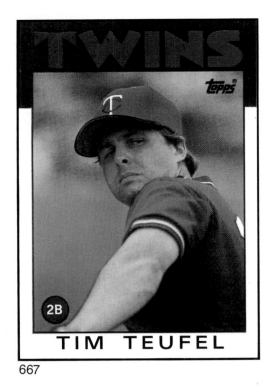

TWINS

TIM TEUFEL

2B

667

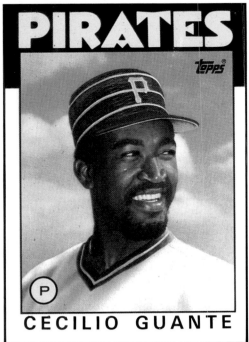

PIRATES

CECILIO GUANTE

P

668

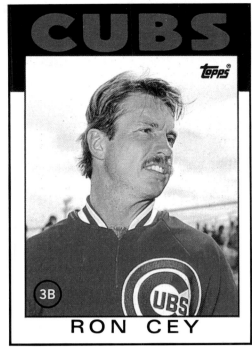

CUBS

RON CEY

3B

669

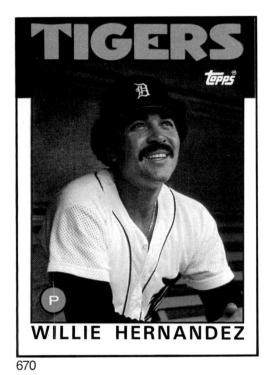

TIGERS

WILLIE HERNANDEZ

P

670

ROYALS

LYNN JONES

OF

671

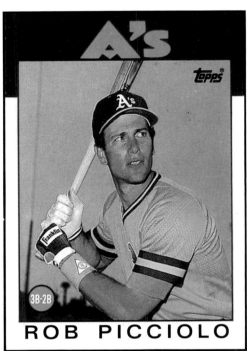

A's

ROB PICCIOLO

3B-2B

672

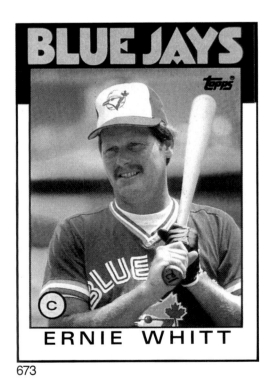

BLUE JAYS

ERNIE WHITT

C

673

INDIANS

PAT TABLER

1B

674

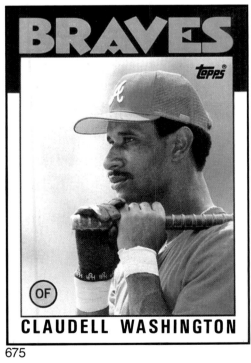

BRAVES

CLAUDELL WASHINGTON

OF

675

A's

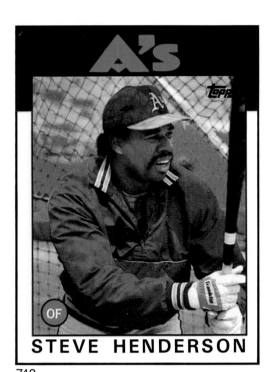

STEVE HENDERSON

748

RED SOX

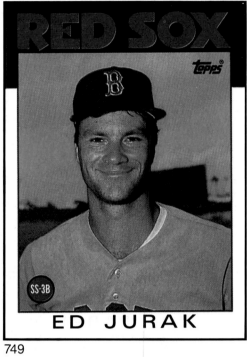

ED JURAK

749

MARINERS

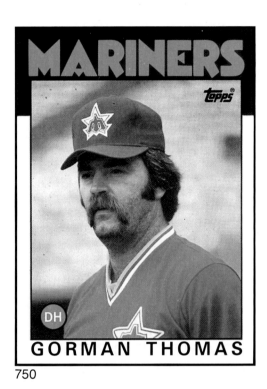

GORMAN THOMAS

750

METS

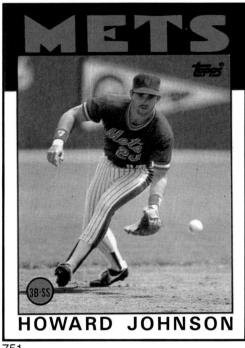

HOWARD JOHNSON

751

GIANTS

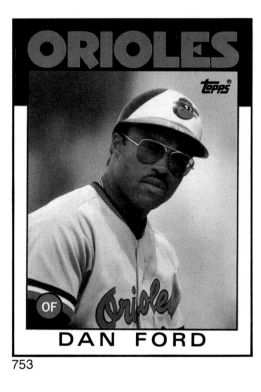

MIKE KRUKOW

752

ORIOLES

DAN FORD

753

PIRATES

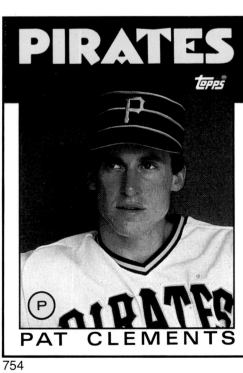

PAT CLEMENTS

754

WHITE SOX

HAROLD BAINES

755

PIRATES LEADERS

756

CARDINALS

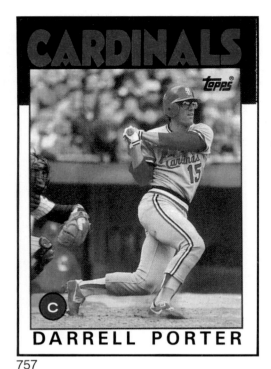

C

DARRELL PORTER

757

DODGERS

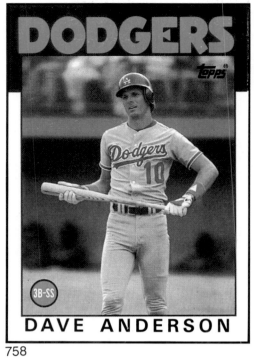

3B-SS

DAVE ANDERSON

758

BREWERS

P

MOOSE HAAS

759

EXPOS

OF

ANDRE DAWSON

760

RANGERS

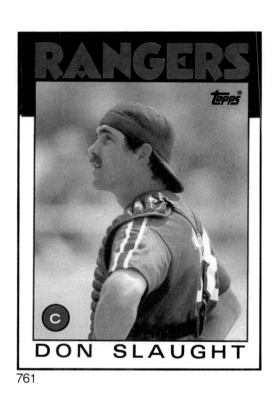

C

DON SLAUGHT

761

PADRES

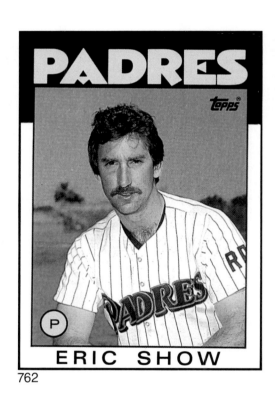

P

ERIC SHOW

762

ASTROS

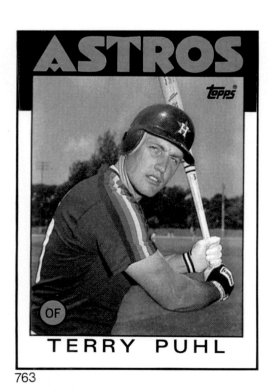

OF

TERRY PUHL

763

PHILLIES

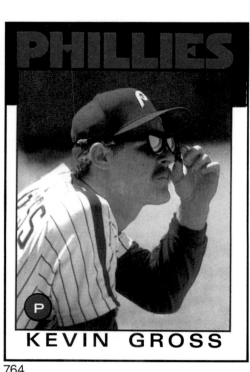

P

KEVIN GROSS

764

YANKEES

DH-OF

DON BAYLOR

765

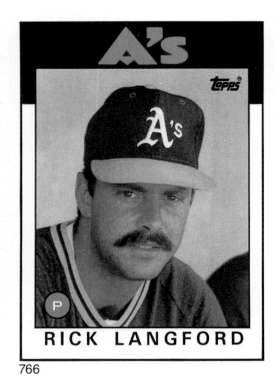

A's

RICK LANGFORD

766

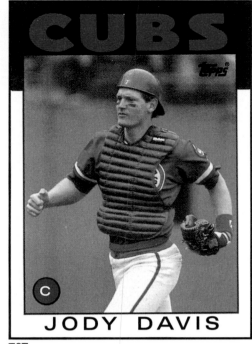

CUBS

JODY DAVIS

767

INDIANS

VERN RUHLE

768

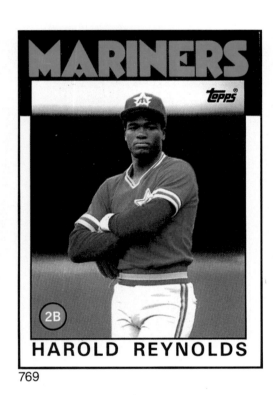

MARINERS

HAROLD REYNOLDS

769

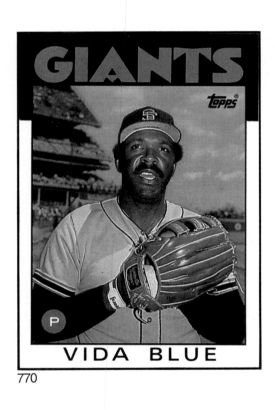

GIANTS

VIDA BLUE

770

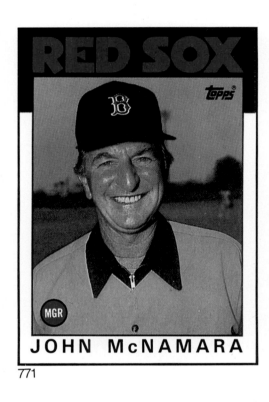

RED SOX

JOHN McNAMARA

771

ANGELS

BRIAN DOWNING

772

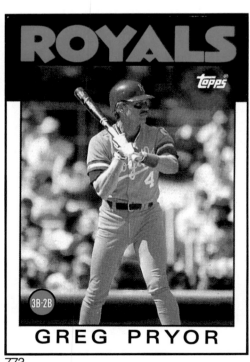

ROYALS

GREG PRYOR

773

METS

TERRY LEACH

774

BLUE JAYS

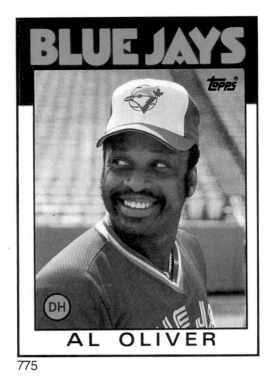

DH

AL OLIVER

775

BRAVES

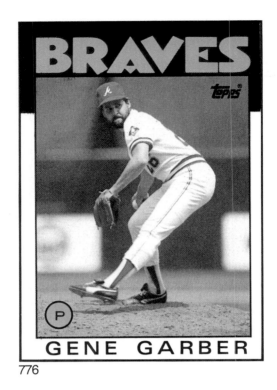

P

GENE GARBER

776

REDS

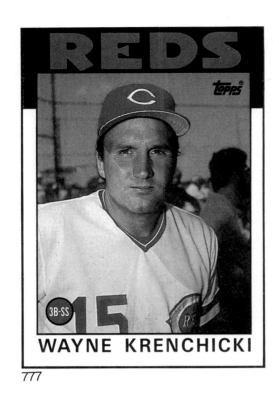

3B-SS 15

WAYNE KRENCHICKI

777

WHITE SOX

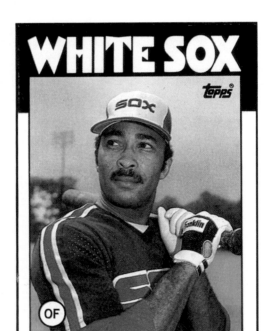

OF

JERRY HAIRSTON

778

PIRATES

P

RICK REUSCHEL

779

BREWERS

OF

ROBIN YOUNT

780

ORIOLES

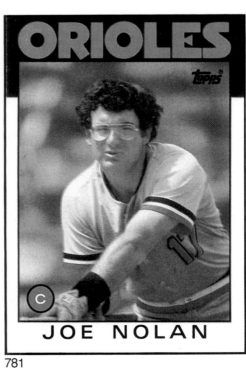

C

JOE NOLAN

781

DODGERS

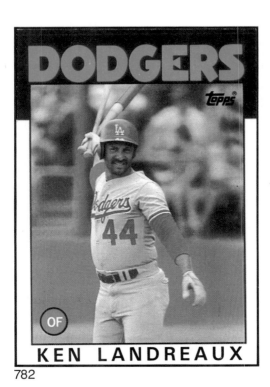

OF

KEN LANDREAUX

782

CARDINALS

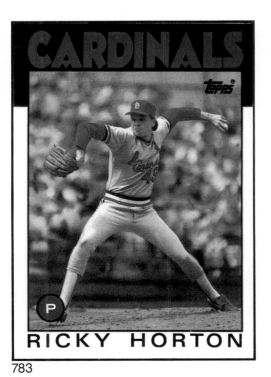

P

RICKY HORTON

783

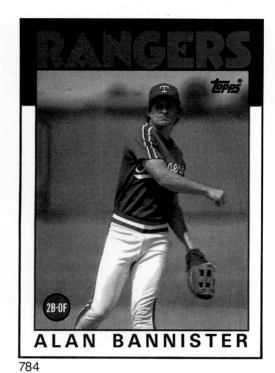

RANGERS

ALAN BANNISTER

784

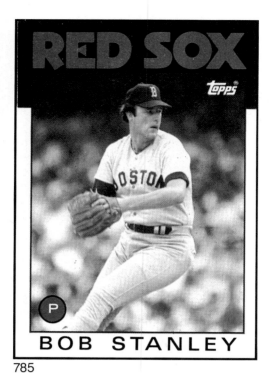

RED SOX

BOB STANLEY

785

TWINS LEADERS

786

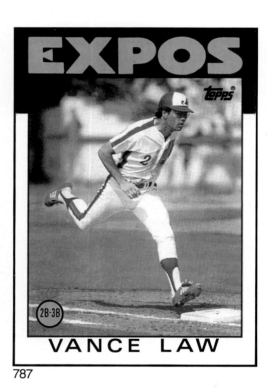

EXPOS

VANCE LAW

787

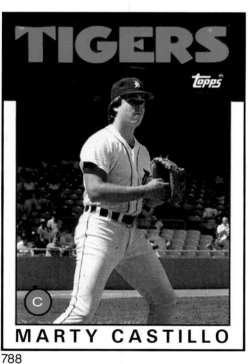

TIGERS

MARTY CASTILLO

788

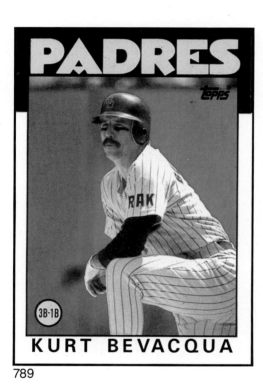

PADRES

KURT BEVACQUA

789

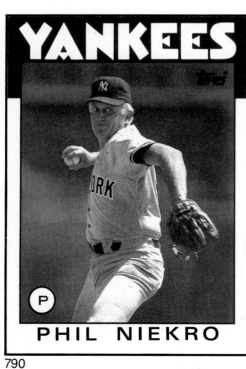

YANKEES

PHIL NIEKRO

790

1986 BASEBALL CHECKLIST
Topps CARDS 661-792

661 ☐ ROGER CLEMENS	693 ☐ TOM TELLMANN
662 ☐ BILL SCHROEDER	694 ☐ GARTH IORG
663 ☐ NEIL ALLEN	695 ☐ MIKE SMITHSON
664 ☐ TIM CORCORAN	696 ☐ DODGERS LEADERS
665 ☐ ALEJANDRO PENA	697 ☐ BUD BLACK
666 ☐ RANGERS LEADERS	698 ☐ BRAD KOMMINSK
667 ☐ TIM TEUFEL	699 ☐ PAT CORRALES
668 ☐ CECILIO GUANTE	700 ☐ REGGIE JACKSON
669 ☐ RON CEY	701 ★ KEITH HERNANDEZ
670 ☐ WILLIE HERNANDEZ	702 ☐ ★ TOM HERR
671 ☐ LYNN JONES	703 ☐ ★ TIM WALLACH
672 ☐ ROB PICCIOLO	704 ☐ ★ OZZIE SMITH
673 ☐ ERNIE WHITT	705 ☐ ★ DALE MURPHY
674 ☐ PAT TABLER	706 ☐ ★ PEDRO GUERRERO
675 ☐ C. WASHINGTON	707 ☐ ★ WILLIE McGEE
676 ☐ MATT YOUNG	708 ☐ ★ GARY CARTER
677 ☐ NICK ESASKY	709 ☐ ★ DWIGHT GOODEN
678 ☐ DAN GLADDEN	710 ☐ ★ JOHN TUDOR
679 ☐ BRITT BURNS	711 ☐ ★ JEFF REARDON
680 ☐ GEORGE FOSTER	712 ☐ ★ DON MATTINGLY
681 ☐ DICK WILLIAMS	713 ☐ ★ DAMASO GARCIA
682 ☐ JUNIOR ORTIZ	714 ☐ ★ GEORGE BRETT
683 ☐ ANDY VAN SLYKE	715 ☐ ★ CAL RIPKEN
684 ☐ BOB McCLURE	716 ☐ ★ RICKEY HENDERSON
685 ☐ TIM WALLACH	717 ☐ ★ DAVE WINFIELD
686 ☐ JEFF STONE	718 ☐ ★ JORGE BELL
687 ☐ MIKE TRUJILLO	719 ☐ ★ CARLTON FISK
688 ☐ LARRY HERNDON	720 ☐ ★ BRET SABERHAGEN
689 ☐ DAVE STEWART	721 ☐ ★ RON GUIDRY
690 ☐ RYNE SANDBERG	722 ☐ ★ DAN QUISENBERRY
691 ☐ MIKE MADDEN	723 ☐ ★ MARTY BYSTROM
692 ☐ DALE BERRA	724 ☐ TIM HULETT

791

PHILLIES

CHARLES HUDSON

792

1951
Major League
All Stars

The 1951 Topps Major League All-Star series is considered by many to be the rarest of all legitimate nationally issued post-war baseball issues. Of the eleven cards, five of the players are in the Hall of Fame: Yogi Berra, George Kell, Ralph Kiner, Bob Lemon, and Robin Roberts. However, two of the three most valuable cards are players who are not Hall of Famers: The Jim Konstanty and Eddie Stanky cards are currently valued at $3,000 apiece. Also found in extremely limited numbers is the Robin Roberts card, currently worth $3,000. These three cards were not issued to the public in gum packs.

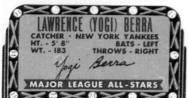

LAWRENCE (YOGI) BERRA
CATCHER · NEW YORK YANKEES
HT. - 5' 8"   BATS - LEFT
WT. - 183   THROWS - RIGHT

Yogi Berra

MAJOR LEAGUE ALL-STARS

LAWRENCE EUGENE DOBY
OUTFIELD · CLEVELAND INDIANS
HT. - 6' 1½"   BATS - LEFT
WT. - 182   THROWS - RIGHT

Larry Doby

MAJOR LEAGUE ALL-STARS

WALTER DROPO
FIRST BASE · BOSTON RED SOX
HT. - 6' 5"   BATS - RIGHT
WT. - 220   THROWS - RIGHT

Walter Dropo

MAJOR LEAGUE ALL-STARS

WALTER (HOOT) EVERS
OUTFIELD · DETROIT TIGERS
HT. - 6' 2"   BATS - RIGHT
WT. - 185   THROWS - RIGHT

Walter 'Hoot' Evers

MAJOR LEAGUE ALL-STARS

GEORGE CLYDE KELL
THIRD BASE · DETROIT TIGERS
HT. - 5' 9"   BATS - RIGHT
WT. - 175   THROWS - RIGHT

George Kell

MAJOR LEAGUE ALL-STARS

RALPH McPHERRAN KINER
OUTFIELD · PITTSBURGH PIRATES
HT. - 6' 1½"   BATS - RIGHT
WT. - 190   THROWS - RIGHT

Ralph Kiner

MAJOR LEAGUE ALL-STARS

JAMES CASIMIR KONSTANTY
PITCHER · PHILADELPHIA PHILLIES
HT. - 6' 1½" THROWS - RIGHT
WT. - 195 BATS - RIGHT
Jim Konstanty
MAJOR LEAGUE ALL-STARS

ROBERT G. LEMON
PITCHER · CLEVELAND INDIANS
HT. - 6' THROWS - RIGHT
WT. - 185 BATS - LEFT
Bob Lemon
MAJOR LEAGUE ALL-STARS

PHILIP RIZZUTO
SHORTSTOP · NEW YORK YANKEES
HT. - 5' 6" BATS - RIGHT
WT. - 160 THROWS - RIGHT
Phil Rizzuto
MAJOR LEAGUE ALL-STARS

ROBIN EVAN ROBERTS
PITCHER · PHILADELPHIA PHILLIES
HT. - 6' 1½" THROWS - RIGHT
WT. - 190 BATS - LEFT
Robin Roberts
MAJOR LEAGUE ALL-STARS

EDWARD RAYMOND STANKY
SECOND BASE · NEW YORK GIANTS
HT. - 5' 8" BATS - RIGHT
WT. - 168 THROWS - RIGHT
Eddie Stanky
MAJOR LEAGUE ALL-STARS

Batting Record & Index

PLAYER	G	AB	R	H	2B	3B	HR	RBI	SB	SLG	BB	SO	AVG	Ref
ADAMS, RICKY	120	247	35	53	5	1	4	16	2	.291	11	37	.215	86/153
AGUAYO, LUIS	266	428	72	113	17	7	14	54	4	.435	44	69	.264	86/69
ALMON, BILL	1046	3034	347	783	125	23	29	263	116	.343	208	566	.258	85/2T, 86/48
ANDERSON, DAVE	259	710	87	157	26	4	8	54	26	.303	92	112	.221	86/758
ANDERSON, SPARKY	152	477	42	104	9	3	0	34	6	.249	42	53	.218	86/411
ARMAS, TONY	1103	4088	502	1022	153	31	213	669	16	.459	206	978	.250	86/255
ASHBY, ALAN	1030	3134	297	754	141	12	62	376	6	.353	336	469	.241	86/331
AYALA, BENNY	425	865	114	217	42	1	38	145	2	.434	71	136	.251	85/3T
BACKMAN, WALLY	448	1388	205	382	59	11	5	98	73	.344	158	211	.275	86/191
BAILEY, MARK	222	676	85	161	30	1	19	79	0	.370	120	141	.238	86/432
BAILOR, BOB	955	2937	339	775	107	23	9	222	90	.325	187	164	.264	86/522
BAINES, HAROLD	847	3184	420	908	153	36	119	501	27	.468	225	450	.285	86/755
BAKER, DUSTY	1956	6875	939	1923	312	23	238	994	137	.436	735	889	.280	85/4T, 86/645
BALBONI, STEVE	355	1238	150	295	56	6	71	188	1	.465	112	366	.238	86/164
BANDO, CHRIS	283	745	80	168	27	2	19	91	1	.344	96	107	.226	86/594
BANNISTER, ALAN	972	3007	430	811	143	28	19	288	108	.355	292	319	.270	86/784
BARFIELD, JESSE	557	1736	264	464	77	17	88	268	37	.483	169	432	.267	86/593
BARRETT, MARTY	336	1071	122	297	50	4	8	103	12	.354	101	77	.277	86/734
BASS, KEVIN	389	1098	136	278	51	13	20	116	26	.378	44	156	.253	86/458
BAYLOR, DON	1912	6961	1048	1843	327	27	284	1085	277	.442	664	855	.265	86/765
BELL, BUDDY	1978	7500	957	2115	363	50	157	918	48	.407	659	646	.282	86/285
BELL, JORGE	415	1488	196	412	74	15	61	211	36	.470	76	220	.277	86/338, 86/718
BENEDICT, BRUCE	725	2227	176	558	77	5	16	217	11	.311	254	182	.251	86/78
BENIQUEZ, JUAN	1264	3995	533	1090	161	29	64	385	102	.376	285	458	.273	86/325
BERGMAN, DAVE	667	1123	137	280	37	9	25	121	13	.365	159	154	.249	86/101
BERNAZARD, TONY	779	2619	362	672	123	24	44	269	85	.372	320	446	.257	86/354
BERRA, DALE	792	2400	223	570	99	9	47	263	32	.345	193	396	.238	85/6T, 86/692
BEVACQUA, KURT	970	2117	214	499	90	11	27	275	12	.327	221	329	.236	86/789
BIANCALANA, BUDDY	156	289	41	56	11	3	3	15	3	.284	24	85	.194	86/99
BILARDELLO, DANN	219	582	49	126	25	0	12	57	2	.321	38	98	.216	86/253
BOCHTE, BRUCE	1413	4826	586	1374	237	20	94	615	40	.401	588	594	.285	86/378
BOCHY, BRUCE	257	600	51	148	25	2	16	60	0	.375	42	133	.247	86/608
BOGGS, WADE	576	2198	367	771	131	15	24	251	9	.457	312	162	.351	86/510
BONNELL, BARRY	959	3017	359	823	141	24	56	351	64	.391	228	374	.273	86/119
BOONE, BOB	1699	5540	507	1403	240	22	89	653	31	.353	490	467	.253	86/62
BOSLEY, THAD	500	1156	137	320	33	10	16	112	40	.364	101	189	.277	86/512
BOSTON, DARYL	130	315	28	67	16	2	3	18	14	.305	18	64	.213	85/8T, 86/139
BRADLEY, PHIL	306	1030	157	307	47	12	26	117	46	.443	97	195	.298	86/305
BRADLEY, SCOTT	28	70	7	14	3	1	0	3	0	.271	2	6	.200	86/481
BRAUN, STEVE	1425	3650	466	989	155	19	52	388	45	.367	579	433	.271	86/631
BREAM, SID	92	208	20	45	10	0	6	29	1	.351	26	35	.216	86/589
BRENLY, BOB	466	1452	182	373	62	5	51	189	23	.412	166	192	.257	86/625
BRETT, GEORGE	1617	6234	1002	1967	400	108	193	977	140	.507	615	443	.316	86/300, 86/714
BROCK, GREG	381	1181	162	275	40	2	55	167	17	.410	177	195	.233	86/368
BROOKENS, TOM	829	2377	282	581	113	28	45	275	63	.372	159	374	.244	86/643
BROOKS, HUBIE	707	2648	263	718	119	18	41	319	34	.376	162	404	.271	85/9T, 86/555
BROUHARD, MIKE	304	909	108	235	40	7	25	104	2	.400	53	184	.259	86/473
BROWN, BOBBY	502	1277	183	313	38	12	26	130	110	.355	94	238	.245	86/182
BROWN, CHRIS	154	516	56	141	27	3	17	72	4	.436	47	97	.273	85/10T, 86/383
BROWN, MIKE	210	610	83	175	40	7	19	84	3	.469	49	91	.287	86/114
BRUMMER, GLENN	178	347	23	87	16	0	1	27	4	.305	25	54	.251	86/616
BRUNANSKY, TOM	601	2172	300	535	103	10	110	309	13	.455	268	386	.246	86/565
BUCKNER, BILL	2023	7795	935	2296	423	44	146	970	169	.416	362	370	.295	86/443
BUECHELE, STEVE	69	219	22	48	6	3	6	21	3	.356	14	38	.219	86/397
BUMBRY, AL	1496	5053	778	1422	220	52	54	402	254	.378	471	709	.281	85/12T, 86/583
BURROUGHS, JEFF	1689	5536	720	1443	230	20	240	882	16	.439	831	1135	.261	85/14T, 86/53
BUSH, RANDY	389	1037	128	247	60	8	36	147	4	.416	97	169	.238	86/214
BUTERA, SAL	224	506	38	120	11	1	3	40	0	.281	56	44	.237	86/407
BUTLER, BRETT	591	2108	350	584	78	39	13	147	168	.370	247	212	.277	86/149
CABELL, ENOS	1581	5675	726	1576	252	56	58	567	228	.373	245	665	.278	86/197
CALDERON, IVAN	78	234	39	65	17	4	9	29	5	.500	21	50	.278	86/382
CAREW, ROD	2469	9315	1424	3053	445	112	92	1015	353	.429	1018	1028	.328	86/400
CARTER, GARY	1557	5573	766	1521	273	24	247	894	35	.463	618	700	.273	85/17T, 86/170, 86/708
CARTER, JOE	232	784	102	204	34	2	28	101	27	.416	36	143	.260	86/377
CASTILLO, MARTY	201	352	31	67	11	2	8	32	3	.301	19	76	.190	86/788
CEDENO, CESAR	1969	7232	1079	2069	434	59	199	970	549	.445	657	925	.286	86/224
CERONE, RICK	790	2580	244	609	112	12	39	286	3	.334	183	262	.236	85/20T, 86/747
CEY, RON	1931	6802	923	1775	301	21	299	1092	24	.443	946	1137	.261	86/669
CHAMBLISS, CHRIS	2077	7448	899	2071	384	42	183	958	40	.415	617	901	.278	86/293
CHAPMAN, KELVIN	172	421	50	94	17	2	3	34	13	.295	33	60	.223	86/492
CHRISTENSEN, JOHN	56	124	12	24	6	1	3	16	1	.331	20	25	.194	86/287
CLARK, BOB	396	967	97	231	34	7	19	100	4	.347	55	199	.239	86/452
CLARK, JACK	1170	4173	668	1158	223	33	185	682	61	.480	580	644	.277	85/22T, 86/350
COLEMAN, VINCE	151	636	107	170	20	10	1	40	110	.335	50	115	.267	85/24T, 86/201, 86/370
COLES, DARNELL	102	294	32	63	14	1	2	17	2	.289	33	55	.214	86/337
COLLINS, DAVE	1244	4065	568	1118	153	48	31	317	342	.359	378	545	.275	85/25T, 86/271
CONCEPCION, DAVE	2210	7936	908	2117	352	46	97	879	301	.359	664	1096	.267	86/195, 86/366
CONCEPCION, ONIX	389	1040	108	248	34	7	3	80	25	.293	47	93	.238	86/596
COOPER, CECIL	1699	6557	941	1990	378	46	223	1014	87	.477	390	773	.303	86/385
CORCORAN, TIM	503	1043	119	283	46	4	12	128	4	.358	128	102	.271	86/664
CORRALES, PAT	300	767	63	166	28	3	4	54	1	.276	75	167	.216	86/699
COTTIER, CHUCK	580	1584	168	348	63	17	19	127	28	.317	137	248	.220	86/141
COWENS, AL	1556	5452	699	1479	272	68	108	711	119	.406	386	641	.271	86/92
COX, BOBBY	220	628	50	141	22	2	9	58	3	.309	75	126	.225	86/471
CRUZ, JOSE	2048	6993	932	2014	350	86	143	960	310	.424	799	872	.288	86/186, 86/640
CRUZ, JULIO	1075	3650	519	871	111	27	23	260	336	.303	436	480	.239	86/14
DAUER, RICH	1140	3829	448	984	193	3	43	372	6	.343	297	219	.257	86/251
DAULTON, DARREN	38	106	15	22	3	1	4	11	3	.368	17	38	.208	86/264
DAVENPORT, JIM	1501	4427	552	1142	177	37	77	456	16	.367	382	673	.258	85/27T
DAVIS, ALVIN	307	1145	158	327	67	4	45	194	6	.469	187	149	.286	86/440
DAVIS, ERIC	113	296	59	69	13	4	18	48	26	.486	31	87	.233	86/28
DAVIS, GLENN	118	411	57	108	16	0	22	72	0	.462	31	80	.263	86/389
DAVIS, JERRY	49	73	13	22	5	1	0	3	1	.397	8	11	.301	85/28T, 86/323
DAVIS, JODY	629	2113	213	539	110	7	76	209	6	.422	185	395	.255	86/767
DAVIS, MIKE	507	1562	223	408	83	9	43	208	76	.408	119	265	.261	86/165
DAWSON, ANDRE	1313	5132	763	1434	263	65	205	760	235	.476	317	817	.279	86/576, 86/760
DAYETT, BRIAN	97	182	18	43	8	1	5	32	0	.374	11	24	.236	85/29T, 86/284
DeCINCES, DOUG	1372	4835	643	1266	267	26	195	719	53	.449	496	741	.262	86/257
DEER, ROB	91	186	27	34	5	1	11	23	1	.398	30	81	.183	86/249
DeJESUS, IVAN	1348	4571	593	1162	175	48	21	323	194	.327	464	657	.254	85/30T, 86/178
DEMPSEY, RICK	1297	3622	396	871	168	11	65	351	16	.347	421	498	.240	86/358, 86/726
DERNIER, BOB	528	1607	259	418	66	10	9	90	158	.330	158	194	.260	86/188
DeSA, JOE	35	55	5	11	2	0	2	7	0	.345	3	8	.200	86/313
DIAZ, BO	584	1857	196	475	99	4	51	271	7	.396	126	256	.256	86/639
DORAN, BILL	475	1758	257	481	64	24	26	145	61	.382	227	216	.274	86/57
DOWNING, BRIAN	1434	4688	673	1245	208	13	146	639	36	.409	694	634	.266	86/772
DRIESSEN, DAN	1676	5379	734	1440	277	23	151	749	154	.412	745	705	.268	86/65
DUNBAR, TOMMY	91	225	19	52	6	0	3	18	4	.298	23	32	.231	86/559
DUNCAN, MARIANO	142	562	74	137	24	6	6	39	38	.340	38	113	.244	85/32T, 86/602
DUNSTON, SHAWON	74	250	40	65	12	4	4	18	11	.388	19	42	.260	86/72
DURHAM, LEON	721	2522	370	717	142	31	96	393	96	.479	310	453	.284	86/460
DWYER, JIM	949	1968	286	504	82	15	48	237	20	.386	276	264	.256	86/653
DYKSTRA, LEN	83	236	40	60	9	3	1	19	15	.331	30	24	.254	86/53
EASLER, MIKE	907	2910	381	852	153	23	99	413	16	.463	252	557	.293	86/477

PLAYER	G	AB	R	H	2B	3B	HR	RBI	SB	SLG	BB	SO	AVG
ENGLE, DAVE 86/43	439	1371	179	368	71	13	28	154	4	.400	98	148	.268
ESASKY, NICK 86/677	323	1037	132	250	41	10	43	157	10	.424	120	304	.241
EVANS, DARRELL 86/515	2135	7254	1097	1825	279	35	318	1067	88	.431	1289	1086	.252
EVANS, DWIGHT 86/60, 86/396	1781	6132	996	1648	328	55	265	852	58	.470	892	1172	.269
FELSKE, JOHN 85/33T, 86/621	54	104	7	14	3	1	1	9	0	.212	9	35	.135
FERNANDEZ, TONY 86/241	264	831	105	235	37	14	5	72	18	.379	62	58	.283
FIELDER, CECIL 86/386	30	74	6	23	4	0	4	16	0	.527	6	16	.311
FISCHLIN, MIKE 86/283	445	839	100	186	27	6	3	65	24	.279	84	113	.222
FISK, CARLTON 86/290, 86/719	1702	6064	961	1666	305	42	267	914	113	.471	597	914	.275
FITZGERALD, MIKE 85/34T, 86/503	228	675	46	150	22	2	8	69	6	.296	65	132	.222
FLANNERY, TIM 86/413	580	1529	159	390	51	18	6	134	12	.324	144	150	.255
FLETCHER, SCOTT 86/187	412	1089	136	267	41	9	8	99	21	.321	116	124	.245
FLYNN, DOUG 86/436	1308	3853	288	918	115	39	7	284	20	.294	151	320	.238
FOLEY, TOM 86/466	263	625	57	150	25	5	8	59	6	.334	56	87	.240
FORD, DAN 86/753	1153	4163	598	1123	214	38	121	566	61	.427	303	722	.270
FOSTER, GEORGE 86/680	1890	6739	956	1861	301	44	334	1197	50	.483	642	1358	.276
FRANCO, JULIO 86/391	485	1883	250	532	80	17	17	252	64	.370	126	196	.283
FRANCONA, TERRY 86/374	365	951	83	276	48	5	7	88	8	.373	36	61	.290
FREY, JIM 86/231				No Major League Statistics									
GAETTI, GARY 86/97	633	2266	270	557	115	11	73	293	31	.403	172	404	.246
GAGNE, GREG 85/36T, 86/162	126	321	39	69	16	3	2	26	10	.302	20	63	.215
GALLEGO, MIKE 86/304	76	77	13	16	5	1	1	9	1	.338	12	14	.208
GAMBLE, OSCAR 85/37T	1584	4502	656	1195	188	31	200	666	47	.454	610	546	.265
GANTNER, JIM 86/582	981	3374	392	930	130	22	33	329	50	.357	215	276	.276
GARBEY, BARBARO 86/609	196	564	72	155	26	2	11	81	9	.387	32	72	.275
GARCIA, DAMASO 86/45, 86/713	809	3227	404	927	151	26	26	255	188	.374	99	260	.287
GARDENHIRE, RON 86/274	285	710	57	165	27	3	4	49	13	.296	46	122	.232
GARNER, PHIL 86/83	1625	5572	708	1460	276	79	95	673	207	.391	505	750	.262
GARVEY, STEVE 86/660	2150	6202	1080	2441	416	43	250	1218	82	.450	455	922	.298
GEDMAN, RICH 86/375	521	1669	195	464	104	12	53	223	2	.450	113	261	.278
GERBER, CRAIG 86/222	65	91	8	24	1	2	0	6	0	.319	2	3	.264
GIBSON, KIRK 86/295	646	2282	349	632	104	30	98	334	106	.478	241	489	.277
GLADDEN, DAN 86/678	246	907	141	256	34	10	12	81	67	.381	78	126	.282
GONZALEZ, DENNY 86/746	61	206	20	43	7	1	4	16	3	.311	20	48	.209
GREEN, DAVID 85/41T, 86/727	475	1368	164	366	46	17	30	179	68	.392	82	273	.268
GRICH, BOB 86/155, 86/486	1910	6577	991	1749	312	47	215	834	103	.426	1048	1224	.266
GRIFFEY, KEN 86/40	1539	5636	914	1689	293	70	100	649	175	.430	565	683	.300
GRIFFIN, ALFREDO 85/42T, 86/566	1066	3814	427	964	136	57	15	285	102	.330	159	339	.253
GROSS, GREG 86/302	1450	3303	412	968	120	45	6	279	38	.362	450	218	.293
GROSS, WAYNE 86/173	1102	3123	374	727	126	9	121	396	24	.395	481	495	.233
GRUBB, JOHNNY 86/243	1284	3830	512	1060	188	28	84	411	27	.406	523	514	.277
GUERRERO, PEDRO 86/145, 86/706	794	2781	441	850	134	21	134	451	75	.513	316	474	.306
GUILLEN, OZZIE 85/43T, 86/254	150	491	71	134	21	9	1	33	7	.358	12	36	.273
GUTIERREZ, JACKIE 86/633	259	734	90	181	17	5	4	50	22	.300	28	87	.247
GWYNN, TONY 86/10	452	1722	245	559	74	19	13	171	62	.412	141	93	.325
HAAS, EDDIE 85/44T	55	70	7	17	3	0	1	10	0	.329	8	20	.243
HAIRSTON, JERRY 86/778	687	1343	170	347	68	6	20	159	4	.363	231	189	.258
HALL, MEL 86/647	300	974	142	267	56	11	29	126	9	.444	103	212	.274
HARGROVE, MIKE 86/136	1666	5564	783	1614	266	28	80	686	24	.391	965	552	.290
HARPER, BRIAN 86/656	175	337	30	82	13	1	11	44	1	.386	10	34	.243
HARPER, TERRY 85/45T, 86/247	367	1072	109	271	37	5	24	133	33	.364	99	190	.253
HARRAH, TOBY 85/46T, 86/535	2060	7113	1079	1891	289	38	188	877	236	.396	1109	815	.266
HASSEY, RON 85/48T, 86/157	680	1990	204	548	96	6	41	273	9	.391	228	206	.275
HATCHER, BILLY 86/46	61	172	25	41	12	1	2	10	4	.355	9	12	.238
HATCHER, MICKEY 86/356, 86/786	647	2226	229	627	120	13	25	238	6	.381	99	156	.282
HAYES, VON 86/420	621	2118	292	567	99	20	50	268	129	.404	212	311	.268
HEATH, MIKE 86/148	758	2530	286	633	102	19	47	289	32	.361	162	322	.250

PLAYER	G	AB	R	H	2B	3B	HR	RBI	SB	SLG	BB	SO	AVG
HEBNER, RICH 86/19	1908	6144	865	1694	273	57	203	890	38	.438	687	741	.276
HEEP, DANNY 86/619	474	1118	120	283	63	3	20	116	8	.369	123	144	.253
HENDERSON, DAVE 86/221, 86/546	551	1786	226	452	95	8	65	227	24	.424	147	344	.253
HENDERSON, RICKEY 85/49T, 86/500, 86/716	934	3463	732	1022	157	34	75	343	573	.425	619	481	.295
HENDERSON, STEVE 85/50T, 86/748	986	3298	439	931	152	49	65	411	78	.417	367	639	.282
HENDRICK, GEORGE 85/51T, 86/190	1812	6557	870	1833	319	26	245	1020	58	.448	520	934	.280
HERNANDEZ, KEITH 86/203, 86/520, 86/701	1572	5539	875	1669	338	57	115	817	94	.445	823	726	.301
HERNDON, LARRY 86/688	1266	4196	524	1152	155	73	86	446	89	.408	280	681	.275
HERR, TOM 86/550, 86/702	721	2603	373	733	120	27	14	288	108	.365	286	247	.282
HERZOG, WHITEY 86/441	634	1614	213	414	60	20	25	172	13	.365	241	261	.257
HILL, DONNIE 85/54T, 86/484	249	725	86	194	26	2	7	79	10	.338	32	66	.268
HILL, MARC 86/552	715	1790	144	401	62	3	34	198	1	.319	184	240	.224
HOFFMAN, GLENN 86/38	645	1849	222	457	93	9	22	190	5	.343	121	261	.247
HORNER, BOB 86/220	819	3054	475	853	138	7	188	565	13	.514	285	417	.279
HOUSEHOLDER, PAUL 86/554	426	1236	140	295	56	10	28	127	35	.368	115	232	.239
HOWELL, JACK 86/127	43	137	19	27	4	0	5	18	1	.336	16	33	.197
HOWSER, DICK 86/199	789	2483	398	617	90	17	16	165	105	.318	367	186	.248
HRBEK, KENT 86/430	612	2266	320	668	129	14	88	383	9	.481	248	334	.295
HUBBARD, GLENN 86/539	912	3165	387	772	147	17	55	329	28	.353	344	439	.244
HULETT, TIM 85/60T, 86/724	155	407	53	107	19	4	5	36	7	.366	31	85	.263
HUNT, RANDY 86/218	14	19	1	3	0	0	0	1	0	.158	0	5	.158
HURDLE, CLINT 86/438	434	1234	143	329	76	11	29	178	1	.417	150	222	.267
IORG, DANE 86/269	653	1541	139	431	101	10	12	205	5	.382	105	159	.280
IORG, GARTH 86/694	672	1813	186	483	95	15	13	164	17	.357	73	199	.266
JACKSON, REGGIE 86/700	2573	9109	1444	2409	437	46	530	1601	225	.497	1250	2385	.264
JACOBY, BROOK 86/116	302	1063	136	284	45	6	27	128	5	.397	80	197	.267
JAMES, DION 86/76	157	456	58	127	20	5	1	34	11	.351	40	49	.279
JELTZ, STEVE 85/62T, 86/453	130	272	24	52	4	3	1	20	3	.239	34	68	.191
JOHNSON, CLIFF 85/63T, 86/348	1262	3609	491	932	176	9	181	644	9	.462	516	662	.258
JOHNSON, DAVE 86/501	1435	4797	564	1252	242	18	136	609	33	.404	559	675	.261
JOHNSON, HOWARD 85/64T, 86/751	323	965	115	245	37	5	30	115	23	.396	97	185	.254
JOHNSTONE, JAY 86/496	1748	4703	578	1254	215	38	102	531	50	.394	429	632	.267
JONES, BOB 86/142	301	582	64	131	17	0	20	83	5	.357	48	112	.225
JONES, LYNN 86/671	460	900	108	233	32	5	7	90	13	.329	67	80	.259
JONES, RUPPERT 85/65T, 86/464	1120	3830	545	966	186	33	122	502	131	.414	450	692	.252
JORGENSEN, MIKE 86/422	1633	3421	429	833	132	13	95	426	58	.373	532	589	.243
JURAK, ED 86/749	160	259	32	70	11	5	1	32	1	.363	33	44	.270
KEARNEY, BOB 86/13	374	1105	103	259	52	2	21	107	9	.342	54	191	.234
KEMP, STEVE 85/66T, 86/387	1139	4006	578	1117	179	25	129	631	37	.433	570	590	.279
KENNEDY, TERRY 86/230, 86/306	821	2941	301	802	155	9	70	420	3	.403	201	491	.273
KHALIFA, SAMMY 86/316	95	320	30	76	14	3	2	31	5	.319	34	56	.238
KINGMAN, DAVE 86/410	1797	6116	831	1457	221	25	407	1116	82	.482	575	1690	.238
KITTLE, RON 86/574	420	1394	196	326	48	3	94	239	12	.477	122	391	.234
KNICELY, ALAN 85/68T, 86/418	194	439	40	95	14	0	11	55	0	.323	51	107	.216
KNIGHT, RAY 86/27	1103	3481	359	957	206	23	56	421	11	.396	244	396	.275
KOMMINSK, BRAD 86/698	215	637	91	137	24	3	12	61	28	.319	72	155	.215
KRENCHICKI, WAYNE 86/777	449	842	86	230	38	3	13	101	5	.372	84	109	.273
LACY, LEE 85/70T, 86/226	1306	3800	538	1099	176	39	73	383	178	.414	303	537	.289
LAKE, STEVE 86/588	121	258	18	52	10	1	4	25	1	.295	5	34	.202
LANDREAUX, KEN 86/782	1046	3636	471	988	163	43	81	427	130	.407	261	354	.272
LANDRUM, TITO 86/498	417	649	81	176	29	10	10	82	12	.393	51	119	.271
LANSFORD, CARNEY 86/134	988	3887	554	1139	196	26	94	491	92	.429	280	473	.293
LaRUSSA, TONY 86/531	132	176	15	35	5	2	0	7	0	.250	23	37	.199
LAUDNER, TIM 86/184	328	943	108	209	51	2	32	110	0	.382	82	263	.222
LAW, RUDY 86/637	662	2114	337	576	75	32	17	162	214	.362	155	188	.272
LAW, VANCE 85/73T, 86/787	612	1908	242	485	91	17	36	213	20	.376	209	295	.254
LAWLESS, TOM 86/228	150	320	38	70	12	1	1	14	25	.272	22	50	.219

PLAYER	G	AB	R	H	2B	3B	HR	RBI	SB	SLG	BB	SO	AVG
LEE, MANNY 86/23	64	40	9	8	0	0	0	0	1	.200	2	9	.200
LEMASTER, JOHNNIE 85/74T, 86/289	1019	3167	317	707	109	19	22	228	94	.290	240	560	.223
LEMON, CHET 86/160	1341	4747	702	1328	281	45	154	613	51	.455	487	692	.280
LEONARD, JEFF 86/490	773	2623	331	713	116	28	75	386	104	.423	201	556	.272
LEZCANO, SIXTO 85/75T, 86/278	1291	4134	560	1122	184	34	148	591	37	.440	576	768	.271
LILLIS, BOB 86/561	817	2328	198	549	68	9	3	137	23	.277	99	116	.236
LITTLE, BRYAN 86/346	293	846	120	212	35	5	3	75	8	.314	114	68	.251
LOPES, DAVE 86/125	1669	6056	970	1591	220	47	147	573	530	.387	777	819	.263
LYNN, FRED 85/77T, 86/55	1425	5192	839	1518	323	39	218	859	62	.496	663	788	.292
LYONS, STEVE 86/233	133	371	52	98	14	3	5	30	12	.358	32	64	.264
MADDOX, GARRY 86/585	1743	6324	776	1799	337	62	117	753	248	.413	321	780	.284
MADLOCK, BILL 86/470	1587	5828	821	1800	313	34	136	743	167	.444	541	417	.309
MALDONADO, CANDY 86/87	296	545	50	129	22	2	11	53	1	.345	44	90	.237
MANNING, RICK 86/49	1369	4929	612	1271	175	39	48	418	159	.338	442	578	.258
MARIS, ROGER 86/405	1463	5101	826	1325	195	42	275	851	21	.476	652	733	.260
MARSHALL, MIKE 86/728	472	1598	199	439	77	3	71	235	16	.460	134	384	.275
MARTIN, BILLY 85/78T, 86/651	1021	3419	425	877	137	28	64	333	34	.369	187	355	.257
MARTINEZ, BUCK 86/518	968	2583	232	589	120	10	56	309	5	.347	210	394	.228
MARTINEZ, CARMELO 86/67	328	1091	136	275	59	3	40	154	1	.422	159	183	.252
MATTHEWS, GARY 86/485	1821	6616	1021	1876	299	50	210	909	180	.439	861	1033	.284
MATTINGLY, DON 86/180, 86/712	410	1546	232	499	107	9	62	288	3	.524	118	106	.323
MATUSZEK, LEN 85/80T, 86/109	272	606	87	139	33	5	21	91	6	.404	66	117	.229
MAUCH, GENE 85/81T, 86/81	304	737	93	176	25	7	5	62	6	.312	104	82	.239
MAYS, WILLIE 86/403	2992	10881	2062	3283	523	140	660	1903	338	.557	1463	1526	.302
MAZZILLI, LEE 86/578	1143	3607	486	950	171	22	81	391	179	.390	537	526	.263
McDOWELL, ODDIBE 85/82T, 86/480	111	406	63	97	14	5	18	42	25	.431	36	85	.239
McGEE, WILLIE 86/580, 86/707	567	2206	314	679	79	45	25	263	162	.418	101	322	.308
McNAMARA, JOHN 85/84T, 86/771	No Major League Statistics												
McRAE, HAL 86/415, 86/606	1954	6908	913	2011	467	66	183	1051	109	.457	625	739	.291
MEACHAM, BOBBY 86/379	277	892	137	208	31	6	3	76	42	.291	90	182	.233
MELVIN, BOB 86/479	41	82	10	18	4	1	0	4	0	.293	3	21	.220
MILLER, DARRELL 86/524	68	89	13	25	2	1	2	8	0	.393	5	19	.281
MILLER, RICK 86/424	1482	3887	552	1046	161	35	28	369	78	.350	454	583	.269
MILNER, EDDIE 86/544	535	1706	265	434	74	22	23	127	115	.364	222	182	.254
MOLITOR, PAUL 86/267	905	3702	614	1080	176	39	70	335	211	.417	324	434	.292
MOORE, CHARLIE 86/137, 86/426	1203	3691	417	968	165	39	32	362	46	.354	312	420	.262
MOORE, JACKIE 86/591	21	53	2	5	0	0	0	2	0	.094	6	12	.094
MORELAND, KEITH 86/266	731	2496	291	721	112	13	71	398	17	.429	242	305	.289
MORRISON, JIM 86/553	730	2207	244	583	105	10	74	263	31	.421	127	323	.264
MOSEBY, LLOYD 86/360	822	2969	424	779	149	41	81	385	129	.422	287	575	.262
MOTLEY, DARRYL 86/332	330	1098	133	278	50	9	37	138	19	.416	55	153	.253
MULLINIKS, RANCE 86/74	705	1940	245	524	128	12	32	228	10	.398	226	280	.270
MUMPHREY, JERRY 86/282	1293	4309	579	1236	185	51	52	490	171	.390	410	580	.287
MURPHY, DALE 86/456, 86/600, 86/705	1200	4403	724	1225	185	25	237	739	122	.493	542	953	.278
MURPHY, DWAYNE 86/8, 86/216	1033	3499	525	865	111	17	136	489	92	.405	580	742	.247
MURRAY, EDDIE 86/30	1362	5129	823	1528	271	19	258	931	52	.509	631	720	.298
NARRON, JERRY 86/543	331	737	59	156	20	1	20	88	0	.323	58	111	.212
NETTLES, CRAIG 86/450	2382	8362	1136	2095	307	27	368	1212	31	.426	1016	1103	.251
NICHOLS, REID 86/364	389	877	125	238	51	6	16	93	20	.398	74	113	.271
NICOSIA, STEVE 85/87T	352	923	86	229	52	3	11	87	5	.347	86	90	.248
NIETO, TOM 86/88	128	339	22	81	14	2	3	46	0	.319	31	55	.239
NOLAN, JOE 86/781	621	1454	156	382	66	10	27	178	7	.378	164	183	.263
O'BRIEN, PETE 86/328	475	1684	192	442	88	1	52	238	14	.420	186	173	.262
OBERKFELL, KEN 86/334	908	2920	346	834	145	33	15	255	47	.373	331	213	.286
OESTER, RON 86/627	827	2845	325	760	126	24	31	240	27	.361	244	446	.267
OGLIVIE, BEN 86/372	1651	5567	753	1517	527	32	230	848	86	.454	530	819	.272
OLIVER, AL 85/88T, 86/775	2368	9049	1189	2743	529	77	219	1326	84	.451	535	756	.303

PLAYER	G	AB	R	H	2B	3B	HR	RBI	SB	SLG	BB	SO	AVG
ORSULAK, JOE 85/89T, 86/102	160	475	66	138	15	8	0	25	27	.356	27	36	.291
ORTA, JORGE 86/541	1628	5443	695	1517	249	61	119	695	79	.412	474	673	.279
ORTIZ, JUNIOR 86/682	143	371	22	90	11	0	1	28	3	.280	13	69	.243
OWEN, SPIKE 86/248	350	1188	144	281	39	17	11	101	37	.326	104	134	.237
PACIOREK, TOM 86/362	1277	3847	471	1084	222	30	79	469	54	.417	241	644	.282
PAGLIARULO, MIKE 86/327	205	581	79	139	31	5	26	96	0	.444	60	132	.239
PANKOVITS, JIM 86/618	128	253	30	65	10	0	5	28	3	.356	19	49	.257
PARDO, AL 86/279	34	75	3	10	1	0	0	1	0	.147	3	15	.133
PARKER, DAVE 86/595	1617	6090	889	1850	366	66	216	977	139	.492	439	946	.304
PARRISH, LANCE 86/36, 86/740	1055	3946	524	1039	195	22	190	638	22	.468	296	764	.263
PARRISH, LARRY 86/238	1490	5365	674	1424	302	30	182	746	24	.435	400	980	.265
PASQUA, DAN 86/259	60	148	17	31	3	1	9	25	0	.426	16	38	.209
PENA, TONY 86/260	657	2362	251	674	114	13	53	288	33	.412	121	303	.285
PENDLETON, TERRY 86/528	216	821	93	219	32	6	6	102	37	.342	53	107	.267
PERCONTE, JACK 86/146	409	1368	185	373	46	16	2	72	76	.334	138	113	.273
PEREZ, TONY 86/85, 86/205	2700	9578	1258	2681	493	78	377	1623	49	.466	900	1842	.280
PERRY, GERALD 86/557	259	624	79	157	19	2	11	66	24	.341	89	70	.252
PETRALLI, GENO 86/296	67	151	10	43	4	0	0	12	1	.311	13	19	.285
PETTIS, GARY 86/604	297	930	154	230	23	17	7	68	112	.331	129	257	.247
PHELPS, KEN 86/34	246	567	81	129	16	2	40	92	5	.474	99	149	.228
PHILLIPS, TONY 86/29	384	1105	150	284	50	10	12	97	31	.353	115	216	.257
PICCIOLO, ROB 85/90T, 86/672	730	1628	192	381	56	10	17	109	9	.312	25	254	.234
PITTARO, CHRIS 85/91T, 86/393	27	62	10	15	3	0	1	7	1	.323	5	13	.242
PORTER, DARRELL 86/757	1629	5254	725	1297	228	48	169	776	38	.405	853	931	.247
PRESLEY, JIM 85/92T, 86/598	225	821	98	214	45	2	38	120	3	.459	50	163	.261
PRYOR, GREG 86/773	726	1771	197	452	81	9	14	139	10	.335	101	171	.255
PUCKETT, KIRBY 86/329	289	1248	143	364	41	18	4	105	35	.363	57	156	.292
PUHL, TERRY 86/763	1074	3914	562	1108	178	50	54	349	181	.396	391	389	.283
RAINES, TIM 86/280	731	2792	513	834	145	45	39	252	391	.425	391	316	.299
RAMIREZ, MARIO 86/262	184	286	33	55	8	3	4	28	0	.283	41	64	.192
RAMIREZ, RAFAEL 86/107	737	2862	308	763	106	20	28	247	68	.347	144	310	.267
RAMOS, DOMINGO 86/462	201	418	42	90	14	0	3	28	5	.270	34	54	.215
RANDOLPH, WILLIE 86/276, 86/455	1353	5019	821	1375	201	53	34	401	218	.355	781	405	.274
RAY, JOHNNY 86/615	653	2474	299	706	150	23	25	259	58	.395	160	124	.285
RAYFORD, FLOYD 86/623	289	784	92	207	39	1	28	95	4	.423	38	166	.264
READY, RANDY 86/209	97	341	50	86	18	8	5	40	0	.396	34	44	.252
REDUS, GARRY 86/342	369	1176	222	292	58	18	31	108	146	.407	172	255	.248
REYNOLDS, CRAIG 86/298	1063	3429	377	890	108	59	29	280	46	.351	158	290	.260
REYNOLDS, HAROLD 86/769	96	173	26	30	7	2	0	7	4	.237	19	24	.173
REYNOLDS, R.J. 86/417	201	632	73	170	27	9	7	77	30	.373	39	98	.269
REYNOLDS, RONN 86/649	54	113	8	22	3	0	0	3	0	.221	9	31	.195
RICE, JIM 86/320	1633	6509	1006	1963	292	72	331	1179	55	.521	502	1140	.302
RILES, EARNIE 86/398	116	448	54	128	12	7	5	45	2	.377	36	54	.286
RIPKEN, CAL 86/340, 86/715	668	2583	431	750	148	19	108	391	7	.488	243	357	.290
ROBERTSON, ANDRE 86/738	254	724	80	182	32	4	5	54	4	.327	26	120	.251
ROBINSON, FRANK 86/404	2808	10006	1829	2943	528	72	586	1812	204	.537	1420	1532	.294
RODGERS, BOB 85/95T, 86/141	932	3033	259	704	114	18	31	288	17	.312	234	409	.232
ROENICKE, GARY 86/494	878	2307	320	575	117	4	108	357	15	.444	339	360	.249
ROENICKE, RON 86/63	348	686	86	170	34	1	11	62	21	.348	111	120	.248
ROMERO, ED 86/317	411	1117	125	287	49	1	5	99	7	.316	88	92	.257
ROSE, PETE 86/1, 86/2, 86/3, 86/4, 86/5, 86/6, 86/7, 86/206, 86/741	3490	13,816	2150	4204	738	133	160	1289	195	.412	1536	1112	.304
ROYSTER, JERRY 85/96T, 86/118	1169	3653	487	913	137	33	28	298	182	.328	350	441	.250
RUNGE, PAUL 85/100T, 86/409	97	214	22	52	7	1	1	11	5	.299	33	40	.243
RUSSELL, BILL 86/506, 86/696	2076	7102	775	1872	282	57	46	609	160	.339	468	644	.264
RUSSELL, JOHN 86/392	120	315	33	75	20	1	11	34	2	.413	30	105	.238
SAKARTA, LENN 86/446	529	1210	154	272	44	3	23	100	30	.323	92	148	.225
SALAS, MARK 85/101T, 86/537	134	380	52	110	21	5	9	42	0	.442	18	40	.289

PLAYER	Card	G	AB	R	H	2B	3B	HR	RBI	SB	SLG	BB	SO	AVG
SALAZAR, LUIS	85/102T, 86/103	647	2129	231	564	79	24	39	232	103	.380	83	355	.265
SAMPLE, BILLY	86/533	734	2316	348	627	116	9	40	216	94	.380	181	204	.271
SAMUEL, JUAN	86/475	339	1429	220	384	68	34	36	148	128	.439	65	325	.269
SANCHEZ, ALEJANDRO	86/563	99	195	27	47	7	3	8	20	4	.431	0	57	.241
SANDBERG, RYNE	86/690	636	2519	426	724	125	34	60	269	155	.435	196	368	.287
SANTANA, RAFAEL	86/587	235	695	56	181	30	2	2	43	1	.318	40	73	.260
SAX, DAVE	86/307	31	46	2	11	3	0	0	7	0	.304	3	3	.239
SAX, STEVE	86/175	617	2437	329	662	75	20	13	174	171	.335	215	236	.272
SCHMIDT, MIKE	86/200	1947	6740	1250	1794	323	56	458	1273	168	.535	1265	1660	.266
SCHOFIELD, DICK	86/311	308	892	93	184	31	6	15	66	16	.305	74	157	.206
SCHROEDER, BILL	86/662	137	477	54	114	16	1	25	57	0	.434	23	138	.239
SHU, RICK	85/104T, 86/16	129	445	66	113	23	5	9	29	8	.389	44	84	.254
SCIOSCIA, MIKE	86/468	543	1594	145	425	73	5	21	173	8	.358	226	107	.267
SCONIERS, DARYL	86/193	234	637	83	169	30	5	15	84	7	.399	48	87	.265
SCOTT, DONNIE	85/105T, 86/568	163	424	34	93	22	0	7	43	1	.321	35	85	.219
SHEETS, LARRY	85/106T, 86/147	121	344	46	93	9	0	18	52	0	.453	29	55	.270
SHELBY, JOHN	86/309	356	950	134	233	36	9	19	86	34	.362	45	185	.245
SHERIDAN, PAT	86/743	328	1021	125	273	45	8	18	106	42	.380	84	194	.267
SHINES, RAZOR	86/132	62	72	0	13	1	0	0	5	0	.194	4	12	.181
SIMMONS, NELSON	86/121	84	281	35	73	13	0	10	36	2	.413	28	46	.260
SIMMONS, TED	86/237	2229	8269	1034	2370	464	47	238	1323	19	.440	807	648	.287
SKINNER, JOEL	86/239	71	135	15	35	6	1	1	9	1	.341	12	33	.259
SLAUGHT, DON	85/107T, 86/16	352	1143	117	322	63	12	15	113	8	.397	60	135	.282
SLYKE, ANDY VAN	86/683	384	1094	157	279	56	15	28	143	83	.410	156	189	.255
SMALLEY, ROY	85/108T, 86/613	1400	4889	654	1256	208	20	135	603	24	.390	667	776	.257
SMITH, LONNIE	85/109T, 86/617	757	2640	491	769	141	30	33	245	273	.405	280	380	.291
SMITH, OZZIE	86/730, 86/704	1164	4225	516	1025	160	34	13	320	272	.306	449	278	.243
SPEIER, CHRIS	85/111T, 86/212	1944	6476	677	1590	268	49	92	638	33	.345	762	859	.246
SPILMAN, HARRY	86/352	319	496	62	112	16	0	11	67	0	.325	46	74	.226
STAPLETON, DAVE	86/151	543	1989	234	545	117	8	41	221	6	.403	112	152	.274
STAUB, RUSTY	86/570	2951	9720	1189	2716	499	47	292	1466	47	.431	1255	888	.279
STEIN, BILL	86/371	959	2811	268	751	122	18	44	311	16	.370	186	413	.267
STENHOUSE, MIKE	85/112T, 86/17	186	395	39	77	14	0	9	39	1	.299	59	61	.195
STONE, JEFF	86/686	148	453	65	140	8	11	4	29	46	.402	24	77	.309
STRAWBERRY, DARRYL	86/80	380	1335	216	348	57	15	81	250	72	.508	195	355	.261
SULLIVAN, MARC	86/529	36	81	11	17	2	0	2	4	0	.309	7	17	.210
SUNBERG, JIM	85/114T, 86/245	1623	5161	537	1306	220	34	71	537	19	.350	587	763	.253
TABLER, PAT	86/674	445	1493	189	412	69	14	23	204	5	.387	149	226	.276
TANNER, CHUCK	86/351	396	885	98	231	39	5	21	105	2	.388	82	93	.261
TEMPLETON, GARRY	86/90	1276	5052	661	1452	219	84	42	475	205	.389	221	687	.287
TETTLETON, MICKEY	85/120T, 86/457	111	287	33	73	14	1	4	20	2	.352	39	80	.254
TEUFEL, TIM	86/667	316	1080	145	286	61	7	27	117	5	.409	126	151	.265
THOMAS, DERREL	85/121T, 86/158	1597	4677	585	1163	154	54	43	370	140	.332	456	593	.249
THOMAS, GORMAN	86/750	1134	4362	636	992	204	12	252	746	47	.453	639	1234	.227
THOMPSON, JASON	86/635	1388	4751	634	1243	200	12	208	778	8	.440	798	850	.262
THOMPSON, MILT	86/517	98	281	33	85	8	2	2	10	23	.367	18	47	.302
THOMPSON, SCOT	86/93	626	1273	132	333	52	9	5	110	17	.328	97	141	.262
THON, DICKIE	86/166	543	1801	234	496	86	23	29	171	92	.397	133	226	.275
THORNTON, ANDRE	86/59, 86/336	1409	4805	735	1240	228	22	236	824	43	.462	801	759	.258
THORNTON, LOU	86/488	56	72	18	17	1	1	1	8	1	.319	2	24	.236
TOLLESON, WAYNE	86/641	427	1225	156	307	32	9	4	50	79	.301	94	180	.251
TOLMAN, TIM	86/272	107	150	14	26	8	0	5	21	0	.327	1	25	.173
TRAMMELL, ALAN	86/130	1138	4057	595	1141	181	35	69	429	124	.394	429	462	.281
TREVINO, ALEX	85/123T, 86/444	583	1674	161	414	68	8	11	160	13	.317	134	196	.247
TRILLO, MANNY	86/655	1499	5381	531	1405	216	33	51	512	54	.342	401	643	.261
UPSHAW, WILLIE	86/745	810	2625	385	713	127	32	88	360	43	.445	254	409	.272
URIBE, JOSE	85/125T, 86/12	155	495	50	117	20	4	3	29	9	.311	30	59	.236
VALENTINE, BOBBY	85/126T, 86/261	639	1698	176	441	59	9	12	157	27	.326	140	137	.260
VAN GORDER, DAVE	86/143	162	389	26	84	12	1	2	37	1	.267	35	55	.216
VENABLE, MAX	86/428	417	814	100	191	29	11	9	65	50	.330	67	117	.235
VIRGIL, OZZIE	86/95	383	1134	131	279	51	5	46	154	1	.422	112	239	.246
VUKOVICH, GEORGE	86/483	628	1602	164	430	76	10	27	203	9	.379	127	229	.268
WALKER, DUANE	86/22	368	839	94	193	36	5	24	96	25	.371	101	183	.230
WALKER, GREG	86/123	428	1367	174	375	85	10	60	229	15	.483	109	226	.274
WALLACH, TIM	86/685, 86/113	705	2251	288	659	134	14	92	335	18	.430	195	400	.258
WALLING, DENNY	86/504	773	1751	233	475	72	23	28	236	36	.387	191	188	.271
WARD, GARY	86/105	726	2738	390	780	139	34	87	368	59	.456	209	452	.285
WASHINGTON, CLAUDELL	86/675	1435	5216	726	1455	259	61	119	635	260	.420	365	970	.279
WASHINGTON, RON	86/513	413	1203	137	321	44	19	13	108	24	.367	52	191	.267
WASHINGTON, U.L.	85/128T, 86/118	825	2652	343	673	103	32	27	245	126	.347	244	379	.254
WATHAN, JOHN	86/128	860	2505	305	656	90	25	21	261	105	.343	199	267	.262
WEAVER, EARL	85/129T, 86/321	No Major League Statistics												
WEBSTER, MITCH	86/629	115	246	43	65	10	3	11	34	15	.463	22	41	.264
WELLMAN, BRAD	86/41	252	625	55	141	23	2	3	57	20	.283	45	114	.226
WHITAKER, LOU	86/20	1139	4120	629	1163	176	43	73	449	82	.399	513	505	.282
WHITE, FRANK	86/215	1652	5534	667	1429	277	50	109	609	162	.385	257	710	.258
WHITFIELD, TERRY	86/318	711	1899	233	536	93	12	33	179	18	.396	133	286	.282
WHITT, ERNIE	86/673	704	1908	218	465	88	9	70	267	13	.409	213	273	.244
WIGGINS, ALAN	86/508	475	1702	279	450	54	16	4	92	201	.322	183	135	.264
WILFONG, ROB	86/658	865	2394	291	604	86	20	35	226	52	.349	188	351	.252
WILKERSON, CURT	86/434	298	879	89	214	23	7	1	49	29	.289	46	140	.243
WILLARD, JERRY	86/273	191	546	60	136	21	1	17	73	1	.385	54	114	.249
WILLIAMS, DICK	86/681	1023	2959	358	768	157	12	70	331	12	.392	227	392	.260
WILSON, GLENN	86/736	521	1774	195	478	100	15	43	232	17	.415	92	303	.269
WILSON, MOOKIE	86/126, 86/315	677	2634	390	724	107	44	31	204	213	.384	136	425	.275
WILSON, WILLIE	86/25	1111	4277	698	1287	156	90	21	313	436	.394	218	564	.301
WINE, BOBBY	86/57	1164	3172	249	682	104	16	30	268	7	.286	214	538	.215
WINFIELD, DAVE	86/70, 86/717	1810	6722	1045	1935	322	66	281	1130	189	.481	714	934	.288
WINNINGHAM, HERM	85/131T, 86/448	139	339	35	85	7	6	3	26	22	.333	29	79	.251
WOHLFORD, JIM	86/344	1150	2955	339	768	121	31	20	294	89	.342	232	359	.260
WOODS, GARY	86/611	525	1032	117	251	50	4	13	110	19	.337	86	187	.243
WRIGHT, GEORGE	86/169	522	1937	209	484	80	15	40	196	15	.369	111	263	.250
WYNEGAR, BUTCH	86/235	1182	3989	467	1029	166	13	57	464	10	.349	579	387	.258
WYNNE, MARVELL	86/525	360	1356	154	332	46	16	9	83	46	.322	98	181	.245
YEAGER, STEVE	86/32	1219	3454	347	789	116	16	100	398	14	.358	330	703	.228
YOUNG, MIKE	86/548	293	889	138	230	41	4	45	135	8	.466	108	223	.259
YOUNGBLOOD, JOEL	86/177	1083	3143	399	843	156	23	69	354	57	.398	286	504	.268
YOUNT, ROBIN	86/780	1671	6515	961	1856	349	75	144	781	152	.428	473	707	.285
ZUVELLA, PAUL	86/572	97	221	18	53	9	1	0	5	2	.290	20	18	.240

Pitching Record & Index

PLAYER	G	IP	W	L	R	ER	SO	BB	GS	CG	SHO	SV	ERA
AASE, DON 85/1T, 86/288	259	875	55	47	399	371	485	343	91	22	5	41	3.82
ACKER, JIM 86/569	131	256	15	8	126	113	119	106	8	0	0	12	3.97
AGOSTO, JUAN 86/657	145	165.1	8	6	74	69	98	68	0	0	0	15	3.76
AGUILERA, RICK 86/599	21	122.1	10	7	49	44	74	37	19	2	0	0	3.24
ALEXANDER, DOYLE 86/196	433	2480	149	125	1114	1012	1060	766	336	77	13	3	3.67
ALLEN, NEIL 86/663	345	680.2	46	56	306	274	451	306	29	5	3	75	3.62
ANDERSEN, LARRY 86/183	241	374.2	10	14	187	161	209	116	1	0	0	13	3.87
ANDUJAR, JOAQUIN 86/150	341	1858.2	110	101	799	715	893	628	256	60	18	8	3.46
ATHERTON, KEITH 86/353	142	277	13	18	124	121	175	104	0	0	0	9	3.93
BAMBERGER, GEORGE 85/5T, 86/21	10	14	0	0	—	—	3	10	1	0	0	1	9.64
BANNISTER, FLOYD 86/64	272	1667	91	103	827	755	1313	632	257	43	13	0	4.08
BARKER, LEON 86/24	237	1278.1	72	75	668	613	953	496	183	35	7	5	4.32
BARKLEY, JEFF 86/567	24	45	0	3	29	27	34	16	0	0	0	1	5.40
BEATTIE, JIM 86/729	194	1108.1	52	81	553	505	636	447	175	31	7	1	4.10
BECKWITH, JOE 86/562	214	403.2	18	19	173	152	306	144	5	0	0	7	3.39
BEDROSIAN, STEVE 86/648	226	572	34	39	227	207	461	267	46	0	0	41	3.26
BERENGUER, JUAN 86/47	137	571.2	28	38	301	265	426	291	82	5	2	1	4.17
BERENYI, BRUCE 86/339	128	742.1	42	53	362	322	577	403	124	13	5	0	3.90
BEST, KARL 86/61	24	43.2	3	3	20	17	41	11	0	0	0	4	3.50
BLACK, BUD 86/697	116	713.1	41	40	333	301	360	203	106	16	3	0	3.80
BLUE, VIDA 86/770	474	3187.1	199	151	1292	1154	2075	1108	445	143	37	2	3.26
BLYLEVEN, BERT 86/445	505	3716.1	212	183	1398	1244	2875	1014	499	200	51	0	3.01
BODDICKER, MIKE 86/575	103	682.1	49	37	284	246	409	241	93	35	11	0	3.24
BOOKER, GREG 86/429	55	91.1	1	3	54	48	40	53	2	0	0	0	4.73
BORDI, RICH 85/7T, 86/94	103	223.2	11	14	106	94	135	63	13	0	0	7	3.78
BOYD, DENNIS 86/605	82	577	31	34	277	249	333	145	75	28	6	0	3.88
BROWN, MARK 86/451	15	38.2	1	2	24	22	15	14	0	0	0	0	5.12
BROWNING, TOM 85/11T, 86/652	41	284.2	21	9	115	107	169	78	41	6	4	0	3.38
BRUSSTAR, WARREN 86/564	340	484.1	28	16	203	189	273	183	0	0	0	14	3.51
BURKE, TIM 86/258	78	120.1	9	4	32	32	87	44	0	0	0	8	2.39
BURNS, BRITT 86/679	193	1095	70	60	499	445	734	362	161	39	11	3	3.66
BURRIS, RAY 85/13T, 86/106	447	2083.2	102	127	1065	949	1023	720	290	47	10	4	4.10
BUTCHER, JOHN 86/638	135	713	35	41	351	321	318	192	95	21	5	6	4.05
BYSTROM, MARTY 86/723	84	435.1	29	26	236	206	258	158	79	4	2	0	4.26
CALHOUN, JEFF 86/534	53	79	2	6	24	20	58	26	0	0	0	4	2.28
CAMACHO, ERNIE 86/509	87	142.2	5	12	59	54	72	60	3	0	0	23	3.41
CAMP, RICK 86/319	414	941.2	56	49	420	353	407	336	65	5	0	57	3.37
CAMPBELL, BILL 85/15T, 86/112	659	1164	80	62	512	451	823	470	9	2	1	123	3.49
CANDELARIA, JOHN 86/140	334	1925	131	87	745	672	1195	451	284	46	10	15	3.14
CARLTON, STEVE 86/120, 86/246	673	4878.1	314	215	1880	1649	3920	1656	655	251	55	1	3.04
CARMAN, DON 85/16T, 86/532	83	100.2	9	5	34	28	103	44	0	0	0	8	2.50
CASTILLO, BOBBY 85/18T, 86/252	250	688.1	38	40	327	302	434	327	59	9	1	18	3.95
CAUDILL, BILL 85/19T, 86/435	399	623	33	48	264	240	580	270	24	0	0	103	3.47
CLANCY, JIM 86/96, 86/412	245	1549	88	102	795	716	813	624	243	58	7	0	4.16
CLARK, BRYAN 85/21T	158	478.1	18	23	260	225	243	241	37	4	1	4	4.23
CLEAR, MARK 86/349	335	615.2	57	39	309	273	606	433	0	0	0	61	3.99
CLEMENS, ROGER 86/661	36	231.2	16	9	105	100	200	66	35	8	2	0	3.88
CLEMENTS, PAT 85/23T, 86/754	68	96.1	5	2	37	37	36	40	0	0	0	3	3.46
CLIBURN, STU 86/179	45	101	9	3	28	26	49	27	0	0	0	6	2.32
COCANOWER, JAIME 86/277	62	321	16	24	179	140	117	163	45	5	1	0	3.93
CODIROLI, CHRIS 86/433	105	537.2	33	32	315	280	245	188	85	12	2	2	4.69
COOK, GLEN 86/502	9	40	2	3	42	42	19	18	7	0	0	0	9.45
CORBETT, DOUG 86/234	256	451.1	20	26	170	152	291	165	1	0	0	55	3.03
COWLEY, JOE 86/427	63	295.1	22	10	136	129	195	132	45	4	1	0	3.93
COX, DANNY 86/294	76	480.1	30	26	210	177	237	141	74	11	5	0	3.32
CRAIG, ROGER 86/111	368	1537	74	98	—	—	803	522	186	58	7	19	3.82
CRAWFORD, STEVE 86/91	104	252	14	10	133	108	120	75	16	2	0	13	3.86
DARLING, RON 86/225	74	489	29	18	201	178	326	235	73	7	4	0	3.28
DARWIN, DANNY 85/26T, 86/519	256	1056.1	61	68	490	425	669	356	119	32	6	17	3.62
DAVIS, MARK 86/138	154	450	17	37	252	231	372	174	58	3	2	7	4.62
DAVIS, RON 86/265	394	633.2	44	44	264	247	510	244	0	0	0	128	3.51
DAVIS, STORM 86/469	129	701	45	28	308	285	390	233	96	25	4	1	3.66
DAWLEY, BILL 86/376	157	258.2	22	13	85	78	155	94	0	0	0	21	2.71
DAYLEY, KEN 86/607	108	265	14	23	150	127	176	93	33	0	0	11	4.31
DEDMON, JEFF 86/129	119	171	10	6	97	79	95	84	0	0	0	4	4.16
DELEON, JOSE 86/75	76	463	16	35	215	199	420	228	68	9	3	3	3.87
DELEON, LUIS 86/286	195	309.1	17	17	115	104	233	68	0	0	0	31	3.03
DENNY, JOHN 86/556	298	1978.1	112	98	878	776	1031	722	295	60	17	0	3.53
DIAZ, CARLOS 86/343	160	232.2	13	6	93	80	189	90	0	0	0	4	3.09
DIPINO, FRANK 86/26	172	253	12	22	117	102	209	113	6	0	0	40	3.63
DIXON, KEN 85/31T, 86/198	36	175	8	5	74	72	116	68	20	3	1	1	3.70
DOTSON, RICHARD 86/156, 86/612	172	1097.2	73	59	514	457	594	441	168	39	8	0	3.75
DRAVECKY, DAVE 86/735	143	660	41	32	247	224	309	185	83	19	5	10	3.05
EASTERLY, JAMIE 86/31	292	563.1	22	30	327	283	319	294	36	0	0	14	4.52
ECKERSLEY, DENNIS 86/538	343	2295	145	117	992	916	1490	581	327	99	20	3	3.59
EUFEMIA, FRANK 86/236	39	61.2	4	2	27	26	30	21	0	0	0	2	3.79
FERNANDEZ, SID 86/104	43	266.1	15	16	100	92	251	121	42	3	0	0	3.11
FILER, TOM 86/312	19	89.1	8	2	46	46	39	36	17	0	0	0	4.63
FILSON, PETE 86/122	126	316.2	14	13	144	139	160	121	24	1	0	4	3.95
FINGERS, ROLLIE 86/185	944	1701	114	118	615	549	1299	492	37	4	2	341	2.90
FISHER, BRIAN 86/584	55	98.1	4	4	32	26	85	29	0	0	0	14	2.38
FLANAGAN, MIKE 86/365	299	1918	129	92	871	811	1079	590	283	92	17	1	3.81
FONTENOT, RAY 85/35T, 86/308	88	421.1	22	21	204	179	182	128	62	3	1	0	3.82
FORSCH, BOB 86/66, 86/322	359	2141.1	129	106	997	871	846	629	326	61	17	3	3.66
FORSTER, TERRY 86/363	573	1064.1	50	64	436	381	763	440	39	5	0	122	3.22
FRANCO, JOHN 86/54	121	178.1	18	5	55	47	116	76	0	0	0	16	2.37
FRAZIER, GEORGE 86/431	311	516	27	33	251	226	325	212	0	0	0	21	3.94
GAFF, BRENT 86/i3	58	126.1	4	5	70	57	60	47	5	0	0	1	4.06
GARBER, GENE 86/776	782	1315.1	83	94	572	487	813	383	9	4	0	170	3.33
GARRELTS, SCOTT 85/38T, 86/395	101	186.1	13	11	84	67	158	113	8	1	1	13	3.24
GIBSON, BOB 85/39T, 86/499	86	242	11	16	127	113	153	142	17	1	1	13	4.20
GLEATON, JERRY DON 86/447	75	154.2	6	10	97	87	62	65	16	1	0	3	5.06
GOODEN, DWIGHT 86/202, 86/250, 86/709	66	494.2	41	13	123	110	544	142	66	23	11	0	2.00
GORMAN, TOM 86/414	112	191	12	9	93	88	128	56	7	0	0	4	4.15
GOSSAGE, RICH 86/530	680	1417.2	96	82	495	441	1212	572	37	16	0	257	2.80
GOTT, JIM 85/40T, 86/463	125	570.2	28	40	306	273	354	234	91	10	3	2	4.31
GROSS, KEVIN 86/764	99	430.2	27	24	198	175	301	160	62	8	3	1	3.66
GUANTE, CECILIO 86/668	149	277.2	8	15	107	92	230	107	0	0	0	16	2.98
GUBICZA, MARK 86/644	58	366.1	24	24	178	165	210	152	57	4	2	0	4.05
GUIDRY, RON 86/610, 86/721	304	2027	154	68	781	715	1510	542	266	88	26	4	3.17
GULLICKSON, BILL 86/299	176	1186	72	61	494	453	678	288	170	31	6	0	3.44
HAAS, MOOSE 86/759	245	1542.1	91	79	754	690	800	408	231	55	8	2	4.03
HAMMAKER, ATLEE 86/223	97	590	30	32	256	226	364	128	91	13	5	0	3.45
HARRIS, GREG 85/47T, 86/586	143	328.2	12	17	148	132	278	136	25	1	0	16	3.61
HAWKINS, ANDY 86/478	105	558	33	29	261	224	230	212	84	12	4	0	3.61
HENKE, TOM 86/333	69	100	6	4	41	37	93	40	0	0	0	16	3.33
HERNANDEZ, WILLIE 86/670	540	808.1	51	45	324	294	592	261	11	0	0	90	3.27
HERSHISER, OREL 86/159	89	437.1	30	11	143	113	312	124	54	17	9	3	2.33
HESKETH, JOE 85/52T, 86/472	36	200.1	12	7	64	52	145	60	30	3	2	1	2.34
HIGUERA, TEDDY 85/53T, 86/347	32	212.1	15	8	105	92	127	63	30	7	2	0	3.90
HOLLAND, AL 85/55T, 86/369	356	598.2	33	30	202	181	471	214	10	0	0	78	2.72
HONEYCUTT, RICK 86/439	243	1391.1	76	96	679	590	549	408	216	46	10	1	3.82
HOOTON, BURT 85/56T, 86/454	480	2651.2	151	136	1112	996	1491	799	377	86	29	7	3.38
HORTON, RICKY 86/783	86	215.1	12	6	83	77	135	73	21	1	1	2	3.22

PLAYER	G	IP	W	L	R	ER	SO	BB	GS	CG	SHO	SV	ERA
HOUGH, CHARLIE 86/275, 86/666	576	1938.1	114	105	848	757	1237	829	160	58	8	61	3.51
HOWELL, JAY 85/57T, 86/115	164	336.2	23	20	161	152	270	123	21	2	0	36	4.06
HOWELL, KEN 85/58T, 86/654	88	137.1	9	12	62	55	139	44	1	0	0	18	3.60
HOYT, LA MARR 85/59T, 86/380	209	1152.1	90	57	537	491	596	211	147	47	8	10	3.83
HUDSON, CHARLES 86/792	94	536	25	32	266	222	317	179	82	7	1	0	3.73
HUME, TOM 86/573	446	908	51	66	430	386	452	307	48	5	0	88	3.83
HURST, BRUCE 86/581	146	829.2	42	46	462	423	520	288	127	21	5	0	4.59
JACKSON, ROY LEE 86/634	252	501	28	33	231	209	319	187	18	1	0	33	3.75
JAMES, BOB 85/61T, 86/467	187	294.2	15	16	126	110	274	117	2	0	0	49	3.36
JEFFCOAT, MIKE 86/571	102	139.2	6	7	59	53	64	49	4	0	0	1	3.42
JOHN, TOMMY 86/240	669	4209	259	207	1754	1513	2055	1129	615	158	45	4	3.24
JONES, AL 86/227	27	28.2	2	1	13	12	19	16	0	0	0	5	3.77
JONES, MIKE 86/514	71	226	11	10	125	111	106	108	25	0	0	0	4.42
KEPSHIRE, KURT 86/256	49	262.1	16	14	136	121	138	115	45	2	2	0	4.15
KEY, JIMMY 86/545	98	274.2	18	11	114	103	129	82	32	3	0	10	3.38
KISON, BRUCE 85/67T, 86/117	380	1809	115	88	839	736	1073	662	246	36	8	12	3.66
KNEPPER, BOB 86/590	298	1887.2	97	106	844	729	1063	580	284	65	22	1	3.48
KOOSMAN, JERRY 86/505	612	3839.1	222	209	1608	1433	2556	1198	527	140	33	17	3.36
KRUEGER, BILL 86/58	75	403	26	26	244	195	175	207	63	5	0	0	4.35
KRUKOW, MIKE 86/752	277	1614.1	88	95	810	711	1103	617	265	27	8	1	3.96
LA COSS, MIKE 85/69T, 86/359	244	974.2	51	54	515	455	401	417	132	17	6	6	4.20
LADD, PETE 86/163	153	216	9	17	114	102	156	78	1	0	0	33	4.25
LAHTI, JEFF 86/33	201	283.2	17	11	109	99	134	110	1	0	0	20	3.14
LAMP, DENNIS 86/219	356	1280.2	72	70	620	546	560	388	155	21	7	31	3.84
LANGFORD, RICK 86/766	244	1436	72	96	696	619	641	398	184	85	10	0	3.88
LANGSTON, MARK 86/495	59	351.2	24	24	184	162	276	209	57	7	2	0	4.15
LAPOINT, DAVE 85/71T, 86/551	151	769.2	42	39	367	324	455	302	119	5	2	1	3.79
LASKEY, BILL 86/603	122	693.2	40	52	352	316	300	191	116	10	1	0	4.10
LASORDA, TOM 86/291	26	58	0	4	—	—	37	56	6	0	0	1	6.52
LAVELLE, GARY 85/72T, 86/622	716	1053.1	78	74	389	332	746	418	3	0	0	135	2.84
LEA, CHARLIE 86/526	127	792	55	40	324	289	462	289	120	22	8	0	3.28
LEACH, TERRY 86/774	64	136	6	6	52	49	76	44	6	2	2	4	3.24
LEAL, LUIS 86/459	165	946.2	51	58	476	435	491	320	151	27	3	1	4.14
LEFFERTS, CRAIG 86/244	178	278	13	14	98	87	164	83	5	0	0	13	2.82
LEIBRANDT, CHARLIE 86/77	138	697	44	33	317	284	267	225	98	14	6	2	3.67
LOLLAR, TIM 85/76T, 86/297	167	863	45	52	424	397	572	446	130	9	4	4	4.14
LOPEZ, AURELIO 86/367	388	794.1	57	32	338	301	570	330	9	0	0	85	3.41
LUCAS, GARY 86/601	334	549	24	38	214	178	335	186	18	0	0	59	2.92
LUGO, URBANO 86/373	20	83	3	4	36	34	42	29	10	1	0	0	3.69
LYNCH, ED 86/68	166	728	38	40	348	310	258	158	98	7	1	4	3.83
LYSANDER, RICK 86/482	137	256.2	9	17	142	122	111	96	5	1	1	11	4.28
MADDEN, MIKE 86/691	58	154.1	11	8	79	67	89	91	20	0	0	3	3.91
MAHLER, RICK 86/437	177	846.1	47	41	373	335	392	266	115	21	4	2	3.56
MARTINEZ, DENNY 86/416	315	1768.2	108	93	894	815	856	581	243	69	10	5	4.15
MARTINEZ, TIPPY 86/82	529	815	55	40	338	302	617	409	2	0	0	114	3.33
MASON, MIKE 86/189	83	397	18	32	211	190	222	139	58	5	1	0	4.31
MATHIS, RON 85/79T, 86/476	23	70	3	5	54	47	34	27	8	0	0	1	6.04
McCASKILL, KIRK 86/628	30	189.2	12	12	105	99	102	64	29	6	1	0	4.70
McCATTY, STEVE 86/624	221	1189	63	63	581	527	541	520	161	45	7	5	3.99
McCLURE, BOB 86/684	359	845	44	42	409	368	504	375	73	12	1	35	3.92
McCULLERS, LANCE 86/44	21	35	0	2	15	9	27	16	0	0	0	5	2.31
McDOWELL, ROGER 85/83T, 86/547	62	127.1	6	5	43	40	70	37	2	0	0	17	2.83
McGAFFIGAN, ANDY 86/133	94	312.2	10	18	139	132	239	96	37	2	0	3	3.80
McGREGOR, SCOTT 86/110	292	1835.2	125	83	834	767	760	419	257	78	20	5	3.76
McMURTRY, CRAIG 86/194	90	453	24	29	222	198	232	217	71	6	3	1	3.93
McWILLIAMS, LARRY 86/425	209	1118	65	56	523	469	692	375	169	29	11	2	3.78
MILLER, RAY 86/381						No Major League Statistics							

PLAYER	G	IP	W	L	R	ER	SO	BB	GS	CG	SHO	SV	ERA
MINTON, GREG 86/310, 86/516	489	778.2	40	48	317	273	309	332	7	0	0	119	3.16
MOORE, DONNIE 85/85T, 86/345	326	523.2	32	31	248	217	324	143	4	0	0	59	3.73
MOORE, MIKE 86/646	119	731.1	37	49	393	365	494	294	115	24	5	0	4.49
MORGAN, MIKE 86/152	64	290.2	10	28	180	168	112	151	45	5	0	0	5.20
MORRIS, JACK 86/270	267	1855.1	123	86	805	745	1104	672	245	95	13	0	3.61
MURA, STEVE 86/281	167	633.2	30	39	311	281	360	289	83	12	2	5	3.99
NELSON, GENE 85/86T, 86/493	106	414	22	28	235	218	235	188	58	6	1	3	4.74
NIEDENFUER, TOM 86/56	235	344	23	22	101	97	285	107	0	0	0	52	2.54
NIEKRO, JOE 86/135	645	3300.1	204	180	1422	1263	1597	1126	447	106	29	16	3.44
NIEKRO, PHIL 86/204, 86/790	804	5054.2	300	250	2112	1814	3197	1648	658	238	45	29	3.23
NIPPER, AL 86/181	57	360.2	21	19	173	156	174	141	51	12	0	0	3.89
NOLES, DICKIE 86/388	197	735	29	46	414	369	389	280	93	3	3	7	4.52
NUNEZ, ED 86/511	129	230.1	10	11	101	91	177	93	10	0	0	23	3.56
O'NEAL, RANDY 86/73	32	113	7	6	49	41	64	42	15	1	0	1	3.27
OJEDA, BOB 86/11	140	718.1	44	39	363	336	425	285	113	20	5	1	4.21
ONTIVEROS, STEVE 86/507	39	74.2	1	3	17	16	36	19	0	0	0	8	1.93
OROSCO, JESSE 86/465	256	437.1	36	32	143	122	366	174	4	0	0	70	2.51
PALMER, DAVE 86/421	122	577.2	38	26	237	209	370	209	86	7	3	2	3.26
PASTORE, FRANK 86/314	187	937	45	57	479	448	523	277	138	22	7	4	4.30
PENA, ALEJANDRO 86/665	107	441.1	25	19	171	140	291	132	55	12	7	3	2.85
PEREZ, PASCUAL 86/491	120	699.2	36	41	347	305	428	212	111	13	2	0	3.92
PETRY, DAN 86/540	207	1388.1	93	64	597	539	717	519	204	45	10	0	3.49
PORTER, CHUCK 86/292	54	236.2	13	13	121	109	136	54	34	7	1	0	4.15
POWER, TED 86/108	208	347.1	24	23	159	144	202	170	12	1	0	40	3.73
PRICE, JOE 86/523	201	618	35	29	262	236	420	217	73	10	1	8	3.44
QUISENBERRY, DAN 86/50, 86/722	444	764	44	35	237	211	259	100	0	0	0	217	2.49
RASMUSSEN, DENNIS 86/301	50	263	12	11	140	123	186	110	41	3	0	0	4.21
RAWLEY, SHANE 86/361	351	1140.1	70	72	532	486	640	460	114	25	4	40	3.84
REARDON, JEFF 86/35, 86/711	394	576.2	35	37	184	168	470	220	0	0	0	127	2.62
REED, JERRY 86/172	57	123	5	7	76	65	64	40	6	0	0	8	4.76
REUSCHEL, RICK 85/93T, 86/93	401	2556	153	139	1089	961	1527	702	380	77	18	4	3.38
REUSS, JERRY 86/577	518	3144.2	192	157	1381	1203	1715	1001	455	123	37	10	3.44
RHODEN, RICK 86/232, 86/756	299	1864.1	106	85	821	738	1018	567	270	48	15	1	3.56
RIGHETTI, DAVE 86/560	220	725.1	50	36	281	249	616	305	76	13	2	61	3.09
RIJO, JOSE 86/536	36	126	8	12	66	58	112	61	14	0	0	2	4.14
ROBERGE, BERT 85/94T, 86/154	125	190.1	12	8	80	77	99	70	0	0	0	9	3.64
ROBINSON, DON 86/731	251	1067.2	56	59	511	461	719	392	126	22	3	17	3.89
ROBINSON, RON 86/442	45	148	8	9	71	60	100	45	17	1	0	1	3.65
ROMANICK, RON 86/733	64	424.2	26	21	208	185	151	123	64	14	3	0	3.92
ROMERO, RAMON 86/208	20	67.1	2	3	48	47	41	38	10	0	0	0	6.28
ROZEMA, DAVE 85/97T, 86/739	242	1094.2	60	53	481	419	445	255	132	36	7	17	3.44
RUCKER, DAVE 85/98T, 86/39	156	266.1	16	16	126	109	140	124	10	1	0	1	3.68
RUHLE, VERN 85/99T, 86/768	311	1363	66	85	650	563	559	341	185	29	12	10	3.72
RUTHVEN, DICK 86/98	349	2098.1	123	127	1066	964	1142	761	332	61	17	1	4.13
RYAN, NOLAN 86/100	581	3937.1	241	218	1571	1374	4083	2186	547	202	54	3	3.14
SABERHAGEN, BRET 86/487, 86/720	70	393	30	17	150	136	231	74	50	12	2	1	3.11
SAMBITO, JOE 86/103T	361	546	33	32	186	159	424	163	5	1	1	72	2.62
SANCHEZ, LUIS 86/124	194	370	28	21	169	154	216	145	1	0	0	27	3.75
SANDERSON, SCOTT 86/406	192	1144	69	58	466	418	759	291	179	29	8	2	3.29
SCHATZEDER, DAN 86/324	273	988.2	52	54	430	397	537	343	117	18	4	4	3.61
SCHERRER, BILL 86/217	180	246.2	7	7	108	98	161	97	2	0	0	11	3.58
SCHIRALDI, CALVIN 86/210	15	43.2	2	3	40	37	37	21	7	0	0	0	7.63
SCHMIDT, DAVE 86/79	172	344	20	22	142	120	203	92	13	1	1	26	3.14
SCHROM, KEN 86/71	110	540.1	31	31	291	266	224	214	75	15	1	1	4.43
SCHULZE, DON 86/542	43	197	7	17	143	124	86	54	36	3	0	0	5.66
SCOTT, MIKE 86/268	175	884.2	47	52	468	409	444	291	148	9	5	3	4.16
SCURRY, ROD 86/449	262	390.1	18	28	156	136	362	234	7	0	0	35	3.14

PLAYER	G	IP	W	L	R	ER	SO	BB	GS	CG	SHO	SV	ERA
SEARAGE, RAY 86/642	80	113.1	4	5	46	43	81	57	0	0	0	8	3.41
SEAVER, TOM 86/390, 86/402	628	4605.2	304	192	1591	1442	3537	1334	619	229	61	1	2.82
SHIRLEY, BOB 86/213	380	1285	66	90	597	520	713	481	155	16	2	15	3.64
SHOW, ERIC 86/762	164	813.1	53	41	338	303	475	306	114	14	7	6	3.35
SISK, DOUG 86/144	167	263.2	10	13	111	88	95	157	0	0	0	29	3.00
SLATON, JIM 86/579	460	2570.1	147	152	1265	1138	1148	964	348	86	22	12	3.98
SMITH, BRYN 86/299	163	649	39	33	255	222	346	192	73	13	7	6	3.08
SMITH, DAVE 86/408	307	470.2	34	22	160	136	291	159	1	0	0	67	2.60
SMITH, LEE 86/355, 86/636	330	508	27	32	178	161	455	190	6	0	0	113	2.85
SMITH, ROY 86/9	34	148.2	6	9	89	81	83	57	25	1	0	0	4.90
SMITH, ZANE 86/167	45	167	10	10	77	67	101	93	21	2	2	0	3.61
SMITHSON, MIKE 86/695	114	779	43	45	375	350	430	216	114	31	4	0	4.04
SNELL, NATE 85/110T, 86/521	48	108	4	3	46	32	48	31	0	0	0	5	2.67
SNYDER, BRIAN 86/174	15	35.1	1	2	28	25	23	19	6	0	0	1	6.37
SORENSEN, LARY 86/744	311	1671.2	90	99	849	766	539	387	230	69	10	3	4.12
SOTO, MARIO 86/725	258	1506.1	89	73	604	549	1337	571	185	68	11	4	3.28
SPILLNER, DAN 86/423	556	1493	75	89	786	699	878	605	123	19	3	50	4.21
STANLEY, BOB 86/785	437	1292	94	70	558	486	483	352	64	17	6	107	3.39
ST. CLAIRE, RANDY 86/89	46	76.2	5	3	36	34	29	28	0	0	0	0	3.99
STODDARD, TIM 85/113T, 86/558	332	465.2	30	26	214	198	378	235	0	0	0	65	3.83
STEWART, DAVE 86/689	210	604.1	30	35	291	266	373	241	55	5	0	19	3.96
STEWART, SAMMY 86/597	307	866	51	45	366	334	514	433	25	4	1	42	3.47
STIEB, DAVE 86/650	222	1654.1	95	80	645	582	942	544	220	84	20	0	3.17
STUPER, JOHN 86/497	111	495	32	28	249	218	191	183	76	9	1	1	3.96
SUTCLIFFE, RICK 86/330	223	1240	81	54	577	514	812	503	164	37	11	6	3.73
SUTTER, BRUCE 85/115T, 86/620	607	976.2	65	67	335	295	805	289	0	0	0	283	2.72
SUTTON, DON 85/116T, 86/335	689	4795.2	295	228	1866	1690	3315	1223	672	174	57	5	3.17
SW'T, BILL 86/599	23	120.2	6	10	71	64	55	48	21	0	0	0	4.77
TANANA, FRANK 86/592	376	2570	147	144	1085	954	1806	707	361	120	27	0	3.34
TEKULVE, KENT 85/117T, 86/326	780	1089.1	74	71	384	327	588	392	0	0	0	172	2.70
TELLMANN, TOM 85/118T, 86/693	112	227	18	7	84	77	94	83	2	2	0	13	3.05
TERRELL, WALT 85/119T, 86/461	91	598.2	34	33	275	243	311	244	90	12	6	0	3.65
THOMAS, ROY 86/626	174	398	19	11	191	166	275	185	13	0	0	7	3.75
THOMPSON, RICH 85/122T, 86/242	57	80	3	8	63	56	30	48	0	0	0	5	6.30
THURMOND, MARK 86/37	89	432.1	28	22	180	154	163	132	70	4	2	2	3.21
TIBBS, JAY 86/176	49	318.2	16	18	145	127	138	116	48	8	3	0	3.59
TROUT, STEVE 86/384	205	1133	69	68	560	482	497	388	175	29	7	4	3.83
TRUJILLO, MIKE 86/687	27	84	4	4	55	45	19	23	7	1	0	1	4.82
TUDOR, JOHN 85/124T, 86/474, 86/710	174	1123.2	72	51	463	416	668	313	162	41	14	1	3.33

PLAYER	G	IP	W	L	R	ER	SO	BB	GS	CG	SHO	SV	ERA
TUNNELL, LEE 86/161	90	396.2	17	24	203	179	224	160	57	5	3	1	4.06
VALENZUELA, FERNANDO 86/207, 86/401, 86/630	176	1285.1	78	57	485	413	1032	455	166	64	23	1	2.89
VANDE BERG, ED 86/357	272	338.1	21	21	159	141	214	145	17	2	0	20	3.75
VIOLA, FRANK 86/742	128	844.1	47	51	455	407	495	271	127	26	5	0	4.34
VON OHLEN, DAVE 85/127T, 86/632	99	146.1	7	4	60	51	52	53	0	0	0	3	3.14
VUCKOVICH, PETE 86/737	280	1422	91	65	647	581	870	534	180	38	8	10	3.68
WADDELL, TOM 86/86	107	209.2	15	10	96	94	112	76	9	1	0	15	4.03
WAITS, RICK 86/614	317	1425.2	79	92	741	674	659	568	190	47	10	8	4.25
WARDLE, CURT 86/303	52	119	8	9	85	81	89	62	12	0	0	1	6.13
WELCH, BOB 86/549	224	1332.2	93	64	513	459	913	424	199	34	16	8	3.10
WELSH, CHRIS 86/52	98	398.2	16	22	218	192	152	149	51	7	3	0	4.33
WHITSON, EDDIE 85/130T, 86/15	273	1182.2	63	64	557	495	656	417	173	16	6	8	3.77
WILCOX, MILT 86/192	381	1958.1	119	105	975	879	1111	742	273	73	10	6	4.04
WILLIAMS, FRANK 86/341	110	179.1	11	8	88	76	145	86	1	1	1	3	3.81
WILLS, FRANK 86/419	40	194.2	9	15	123	119	111	96	27	1	0	1	5.50
WINN, JIM 86/489	46	105.1	4	6	62	61	36	46	7	0	0	1	5.21
WOJNA, ED 86/211	15	42	2	4	35	27	18	19	7	0	0	0	5.79
YOUMANS, FLOYD 86/732	14	77	4	3	27	21	54	49	12	0	0	0	2.45
YOUNG, CURT 86/84	47	163.2	9	9	108	102	65	58	26	2	1	0	5.61
YOUNG, MATT 86/676	92	535.1	29	42	302	265	369	212	89	11	4	1	4.46
ZAHN, GEOFF 86/42	304	1848.2	111	109	889	769	705	526	270	79	20	1	3.74

STATISTICS 1951 MAJOR LEAGUE ALL STARS

BATTING RECORD

PLAYER	G	AB	R	H	2B	3B	HR	RBI	SB	SLG	BB	SO	AVG
BERRA, YOGI	2120	7555	1175	2150	321	49	358	1430	30	.482	704	414	.285
DOBY, LARRY	1533	5348	960	1515	243	52	253	969	47	.490	871	1011	.283
DROPO, WALT	1288	4124	478	1113	168	22	152	704	5	.432	328	582	.270
EVERS, HOOT	1142	3801	556	1055	187	41	98	565	45	.426	415	420	.278
KELL, GEORGE	1795	6702	881	2054	385	50	78	870	51	.414	620	287	.306
KINER, RALPH	1472	5205	971	1451	216	39	369	1015	22	.548	1011	749	.279
RIZZUTO, PHIL	1661	5816	877	1588	239	62	38	563	149	.355	650	397	.273
STANKY, EDDIE	1259	4301	811	1154	185	35	29	364	48	.348	996	374	.268

PITCHING RECORD

PLAYER	G	IP	W	L	SO	BB	GS	CG	SHO	SV	ERA
KONSTANTY, JIM	433	947	66	48	268	269	36	14	2	74	3.46
LEMON, BOB	460	2849	207	128	1277	1251	350	188	31	22	3.23
ROBERTS, ROBIN	676	4689	286	245	2357	902	609	305	45	25	3.40

YANKEES

1B

DON MATTINGLY

BLUE JAYS

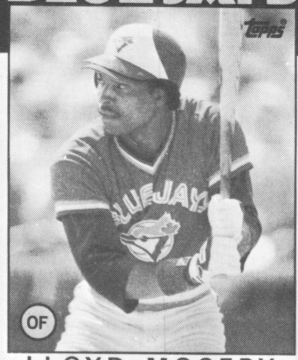

OF

LLOYD MOSEBY

WHITE SOX

P 50

TOM SEAVER

CARDINALS

OF

VINCE COLEMAN

ASTROS

P Astros

NOLAN RYAN

DODGERS

OF

PEDRO GUERRERO

METS

OF

DARRYL STRAWBERRY

DODGERS

MGR

TOM LASORDA

METS

C

GARY CARTER